The Best Things in Life Are Free

The Best Things in Life Are Free

TODD OUTCALT

Health Communications, Inc.
Deerfield Beach, Florida

www.hci-online.com

Library of Congress Cataloging-in-Publication Data

Outcalt, Todd.
    The best things in life are free / Todd Outcalt.
        p.   cm.
    ISBN 1-55874-607-2 (pbk.)
    1. Conduct of life.   I. Title
    BJ1597.098   1998
    170'.44—dc21   98-16010
                                                                            CIP

© 1998 Todd Outcalt

ISBN 1-55874-607-2

Publisher: Health Communications, Inc.
                 3201 S.W. 15th Street
                 Deerfield Beach, FL 33442-8190

Cover design by Lawna Patterson Oldfield
Cover illustration ©Artville

To my parents,

who have given me the best things in life

CONTENTS

Part Four: Moments to Treasure

Part Five: The End of the Day

ACKNOWLEDGMENTS

This is a book about the small gifts of life. As such, the book itself is a gift, for writing it challenged me and offered me far more than I anticipated. I'm grateful to have persevered and seen it through to fruition.

Any book owes its existence to the people who have a love for writing and who work to offer the book to the public. To this end I thank Peter Vegso, Christine Belleris and all the visionaries at Health Communications, Inc., who not only produce beautiful books, but have looked after my own interests as much as theirs, and included me in the undertaking at every step. A special thanks to Matthew Diener for his editorial expertise and fine suggestions on improving the manuscript. He made a better book out of my words, and all the deficiencies are mine. Thanks also to Erica Orloff and Lisa Drucker.

As always, I am blessed with the usual cast of characters who make each day a joy and a miracle. I thank my wife, Becky, for giving so much of herself and taking up most of the family slack during the evenings I worked on this book. And I am inexpressibly happy to be father and friend to two wonderful children, Chelsey and Logan.

I cannot begin to thank the long line of family and friends who have contributed in one way or another to the stories in this volume. The fact that they have been, and are, an integral part of my life means more than I can say. You are the gift, and I am the recipient.

All of you have added much to the best things in my life.

INTRODUCTION

Over the years, I've come to believe that there are two basic types of people in the world: those who believe that happiness is beyond them, and those who are happy. I've also heard it said that good things come to those who wait and that nice guys finish last. I'm not sure about either of those propositions. But I can say that I believe that the best things in life are free.

I've spent a great deal of time thinking about these things and talking about them with others, and I've come to a few conclusions that might ring true for a great many people:

We value family and friends and children more than
  things.
We all want to love and be loved.
We'd rather laugh than cry.
An actual sunset is more awesome than a picture of a
  sunset.
We all want to achieve something in life.

We cherish our memories more than our knowledge.
We desire to help others.
We all hope and believe in something or someone
    greater than ourselves.
Rest is more satisfying after a hard day's work.

If you've ever felt this way or entertained these thoughts, then
you are probably quite content or you are working hard to find
life's joy. You'll discover many such sentiments expressed within
these pages, for you'll no doubt find that the best things in *your*
life are free.

Just the other day I conducted a little experiment on myself
to test this theory—a kind of self-assessment (which you might
want to try out on your partner). I walked around my house
and my office, identifying ten important artifacts that I valued
deeply, scribbling each one onto a Post-it Note. I then retreated
into my office and proceeded to rank them in order of importance or value by sticking them on the wall, from highest to
lowest—my own top ten list of most cherished items.

Here was my list:

1. Master's diploma from Duke University (representative
   of working my buns off for three years in a vain attempt
   to disprove the fact that I know nothing).

2. Bank account (representative of a lifetime of work for
   little pay).

3. Personal wardrobe (no explanation necessary).

4. Automobile with 108,000 miles (more valuable than
   bicycle in garage).

5. Personal library (representative of a lifetime of knowing nothing).

6. Personal computer (representative of the fact that I once got a D in typing but have overcome the odds with the help of superior technology).

7. Guitar collection (representative of the fact that I know nothing about music).

8. Award plaque (don't remember how I got it but looks prestigious hanging on office wall).

9. Bed (perfect place to sleep and make love to my wife— would have ranked higher earlier in marriage).

10. Kitchen table (best place to eat—might have doubled as most desired place to make love to my wife earlier in marriage).

Once I had my list in order, I sat down and did some thinking. Serious thinking. Which of these items, I asked myself, would be indispensable in the event of an all-out nuclear attack? I gathered I could get along quite well without the guitars and the kitchen table. My award plaque could double as a shaving mirror. I could sleep on the floor if necessary.

Next, I asked myself a far more penetrating question: Which of these items did I value more than family and friends? Nothing on the list came close.

Then I started thinking about all the things I had not included in my list, other items that meant a great deal to me, and I realized that my life was composed of far more than cars and furniture and books and computers. I thought about a box I had stashed in the attic years ago—a box filled with childhood memorabilia—and I realized I wouldn't want to give that up. . . . It holds too many great memories. I thought about all the friends I had, and all the laughter I've experienced, and the good health I've enjoyed. Can't do without these. I thought about the places I've been, and the beauty I've seen, and the people I've known—and I came to realize that my list of "stuff" didn't really define *me* at all.

Oh, some of these "things" are sources of great pride—like the diploma and the plaque (and sometimes the bed when I'm really in the mood), but they are merely representative of something I have already accomplished. They are symbols of deeper realities.

I imagine that you would discover the same about your life if you took the time to participate in this little exercise. Make your list. Check it twice. Compare what you have with what you truly love, and you'll find that the old saying holds true: The best things in your life are free.

Or, if you want to get at this truth from another angle, try the yellow pages in your telephone book. I'm a big believer that the yellow pages tell us a great deal more about people than most books do. The yellow pages provide a glimpse into the human experience, the thought processes by which most of us live out our days and try to make sense of this thing we call "life."

Get your phone book out and see if you can't follow along.

Riffle through the As, and you'll find listings for *Ambulance* and *Art*. You'll also find a section for *Attorneys*. In my phone book the *Attorneys* section is nearly eighty pages thick (more massive, by far, than any other section, including *Dentists* and *Physicians*, and *Churches* and *Synagogues*). There are also listings for *Funeral Directors*, *Heating*, *Insurance*, *Lawn* and *Loans*. *Financing* and *Fire* are close together, as are the sections for *Humane Societies* and *Hunting*. The *Marriage* section is thin—a mere four pages—but you can find longer sections on *Motels* and *Movers* in case you are in that vein of thought. I notice that the *Pawnbroker* section is getting thicker every year, as are the sections on *Palmists* and *Psychic Mediums*, while the *Radio* and *Rubber Stamps* sections seem to be declining. Need help around the house? Try *Plumbing* (another massive section, often with subheadings!) or *Rental* or *Septic*. Eventually you'll come to *Water* and *Waterproofing*. And a few pages later you'll end up looking at *Yogurt, Zippers* and *Zoos*.

That's life according to the yellow pages. But what do those pages tell us about you and me?

Well, first of all, they tell us that those headings were not created by accident. You and I tend to think about life in terms of personal needs and sudden crises. We run into trouble with money, and we might turn to *Financing, Loans* or *Psychic Mediums*. Something gives us a bellyache, and we look up *Physician* or *Pharmacy*. Most of the yellow page headings are there to meet the major crises of our lives.

Now, the opposite is also true. There are a great many things you won't find in the yellow pages, even though they may be major factors in life. For example, you won't find a section on *Love* or *Faith*. You are not likely to find headings for *Volunteer Opportunities* or *Friendship*. And sorry, there is nothing at all on *Hope* or *Laughter*.

To find these things you have to dig deep into yourself. You have to look and listen and learn. You have to be willing to be vulnerable and experience what life has to give.

The yellow pages also remind us that we tend to categorize or compartmentalize life. We tend to divide ourselves into pieces—husband or wife, son or daughter, healthy or sick, wealthy or needy, take-out or eat-in. Marketing folks know this. They accommodate us by giving us what we ask for—

little snippets of life to go with our little snippets of time. All alphabetized. All readily available. All a phone call away.

If you want to test these theories, just hang out by the pay phones at any bus stop, airport or mall. You'll be amazed at how many people thumb through the yellow pages looking for one answer or another before they step toward a bus, board an airplane or begin a day of shopping. God only knows what they are looking for (or what any of us are looking for). But there they are, dropping quarters and dimes and nickels into the slot, reaching out for an answer. The problem may be a clogged drain or postnasal drip, a death in the family or a hunger pang. But someone with a yellow page listing is getting the call.

What does all of this have to do with appreciating the little things of life? Not much. Or maybe everything. For most everyone will admit that the best things often happen to us when we are not aware of them. Happiness and love and laughter find us through the cracks of life. And wouldn't it be wonderful if, just once, we could see the *big picture* instead of experiencing life as a series of disjointed days and nights, a series of unrelated events?

That's what this book is about. Think of it as a kind of yellow pages for the soul. You don't have to go anywhere or be anything to experience these joys. You don't have to have a crisis. All you need to do is take what life has given you for free.

Like most books of a personal nature, folks will naturally want to know whether this book contains any true stories. All my stories are true, although there are some that, because they happened long ago or may be too painful to remember any other way, may be tinged with some favorable nostalgia and poetic license. I have also changed some names to pro-tect identities—usually my own. But all the people are real, and I hope they will remind you of the family and friends who have touched *your* life.

Somewhere in your reading you may also discover that this little volume seems to be saying the same thing over and over, but in different ways. Reading about *Children,* you may find yourself thinking of *Memories* or *Family.* Reading about *Laughter,* you may be reminded of *Simple Pleasures* or *Good Health.* Wonderful. Let it be.

Further on, as you near the end of this book, I hope you will consider passing it on to a friend or someone you love. Or give some aspect of yourself away. Make a card, write a letter. After all, the best things in life are free.

PART ONE

···

The People in
Our Lives

1

Family

*All happy families resemble
one another. . . .*

—Leo Tolstoy, *Anna Karenina*

When I was four years old, my best friend was Alan. He lived across the street in a house shaded by maple trees and overgrown shrubs. We were average boys—getting into all the trouble that four-year-old boys typically get into—but even then I knew there was something quite different about our families.

My family lived in a small, white board house kept in prime condition by my father, who was a barber. Dad had renovated the front porch into a shop where, for eight hours each day, six days a week, he cut men's hair for a dollar a scalp. Crew cuts and flat tops were the style in those days, and my hair was always cropped close to the skin. It was years before I discovered that I even *had* hair. Because the house doubled as my father's business, the lawn was always neatly trimmed, the fence painted, and the shutters on the windows were kept spotless and neat. I saw my father every day. When my mother returned from school (she was a teacher), we always sat down to dinner together with my baby brother and said a prayer. Afterward we spent the evening together as a family.

But, even at four years of age, I knew Alan's situation was quite different from my own. I could sense these differences, although I could not name them.

Alan lived in a house on the corner that was not as neatly tended as the house my family occupied. Some of the windows were cracked. The grass in the yard was unkempt, and there were patches of dirt and sand, where we often played with toy soldiers. The siding on the house was flaking and badly in need of paint, and the front porch tilted to one side.

Unlike my parents, who were healthy and strong, Alan's parents were not so fortunate. His mother had cerebral palsy, and I observed that it was difficult for her to do even the simplest chores, the basic household work that my mother did with relative ease. Cooking and laundry and cleaning were demanding efforts for Alan's mother. Nothing came easily.

Alan had a sister who had been born with the same affliction as his mother. She was confined to a wheelchair, and, unlike my baby brother who crawled around the house and took to the stairs with reckless abandon, she rarely moved beyond the confines of the tiny living room.

Unlike my father, who was always near, I was aware that Alan's father was frequently absent. He spent much of his time in a place called "the pen." It was later in life that I learned that his father spent days, sometimes weeks at a time, in the county jail. He was an alcoholic who had fallen deeply into the clutches of his disease and was unable to find a way out of the black hole of despair.

Before I turned six, our family moved upstate, taking up residence in a larger city. The day we packed up and left was the last time I saw Alan.

Over the years I have thought much about this childhood friend and his family. And, like most early acquaintances, from time to time I have caught glimpses of newspaper clippings and heard snippets of conversation which have filled in the gaps of our lives. Alan's father died before Alan graduated from high school. His sister soon followed. His mother spent the remaining years of her life in a nursing facility being cared for by strangers. The last I knew, Alan had joined the military, was discharged and was working as a mechanic.

Of all the inequalities in life, the inequalities of our family relationships seem to me the cruelest. Why should some of us be blessed with a stable childhood, a set of loving parents, a home filled with love? Why should other children be forced to endure the ravages of poverty or alcoholism, divorce or death, or the longing for absent parents?

Of course there are no answers, but when we ask the difficult questions, I believe we discover that for which we search. I've known many people who have not only endured a difficult childhood, but emerged triumphant from their circumstances. These people have dedicated themselves to providing a better home for their own children or making a better life for themselves. Others who have endured hardship realize

that a family should never be taken for granted, and they recognize that hard work is required to make any house a home.

When I consider my own family, I know this is true. Our
family has seen good times and bad, endured and persevered,
but it is the qualities of love and faith that have served to
hold life together through the rough spots. Sometimes the
adversity itself has served to inspire our family and cause us
to rally together. Families with carefree lives can become
unstable and unhappy. Overcoming challenges and problems
can be a source of great strength to people who love each
other and are looking toward a better tomorrow.

Difficulties also cause us to look back, to see how far we
have come.

A family is a unit with a history. And every family likes to
know its roots. By looking to the past, we sometimes gain a
vision of where we are going. I suppose that is why folks like
to dig into genealogies, why they like to sift through old
courthouse records and thumb through the family Bible.
Family history is a kind of social archaeology—digging up the
past in family heirlooms and remnants, searching for clues
that might indicate why things turned out the way they did.

Back in the 1970s, after Alex Haley wrote his epic family
saga, *Roots,* many Americans suddenly found a renewed
interest in genealogy. Folks were fascinated by their own
roots and wanted to learn about their ancestors. I suppose
that, by searching for their roots, many families found a new
identity for being and belonging. They came to believe that
the past might hold the key to the future.

Several years ago, I received an unexpected phone call
from a woman bearing my same family name. She lived on

the other side of town and invited me to bring my genealogy to her family reunion "to see how we are related." A quick comparison of our family histories revealed that my great-great-grandfather and her great-great-grandfather had been brothers. They had lived in the Wisconsin region, in an old German community, and had parted ways in the late 1870s. Over the years the family name was transformed through several spelling changes, mostly attempts at simplification, and it finally eroded into an abbreviated form of the original German spelling. Like most names before the age of accurate public records, people wrote a name the way it sounded. Thus, the name was changed forever.

As far as I know, we were a German-speaking bunch way back when, but you'd never know it now. My grandmother Outcalt (who is, of course, only an Outcalt by marriage) evokes nothing of this German heritage, except maybe in her ironclad will, good humor and good looks.

When I consider all the things my grandmother taught me, certain games come to mind—games like hide-the-thimble and handy-andy-over and who's-got-the-button and riddle-me-riddle-me-ree. I grew up on these simple Sunday afternoon games, and they were fun. I blush when I think about all the extravagant toys and games I have purchased for my children. They play with the games a time or two and then relegate them to the closet. But the simple games my grandmother taught me years ago . . . these games never go out of style. My children love them, too.

My grandmother also has a contagious laugh, and some of my fondest memories center on the humor our family has shared together over bowls of popcorn or a bucket of homemade ice cream. A good laugh—even to the point of tears—never did anyone harm, and I like to think that laughter keeps a family healthy. When a family is laughing together, they don't have time to worry about their problems or stew about all the things that *might* happen.

As for the maternal side of my family, my grandfather Neeley has always been something of an anomaly—nearly ninety years old, healthy as a kid, still mowing his lawn with a push-mower. For most of his adult life, he ran a small general store in the tiny town of Heathsville, Illinois—population ten—a hamlet named after the infamous candy-bar manufacturer who made a name for himself in the English-toffee business with the candy bar that still bears his name: Heath.

Growing up, I spent many afternoons and evenings roaming around the store, inspecting the goods, yearning for a candy bar and a bottle of pop. Grandpa's shelves were littered with such sweet temptations as well as canned foods and fresh vegetables. There were also dry goods: bolts of fabric, hardware supplies, hand tools, batteries, and health and beauty items. In the back a refrigerated meat counter was filled with wheels of cheese, blocks of cold cuts, eggs and fish. The meat was sliced on a machine with a rotating wheel and weighed on a scale, and the sandwiches people ordered were made by hand. In the basement, my grandpa had a creamery. Folks brought in their milk and cream, and exchanged these goods for other items.

General stores like my grandfather's represented the last of the barter-and-exchange system in our culture. These small general stores sprinkled around the countryside were like community centers, places where people gathered to meet and discuss the state of politics and world events, and exchange the latest gossip—naturally, with a bottle of pop in hand.

But, like the small farms, the small general stores went by the wayside when larger discount stores and corporations sprung up, offering a wider range of goods at a lower cost. Today, we call these general stores by different names— Wal-Mart and Kmart, for example—but the old country stores were simply a smaller variation of these giants. Everything was available under one roof.

I happen to know that these little general stores also kept people alive during the tough times. Proprietors like my grandpa knew folks by name, gave out food and clothing on an IOU and a promise, and never recovered many of the debts people placed "on their tabs." Operating a general store required a knowledge and love of people, and much wisdom and savvy.

Once, when my grandfather was a young man and just starting out in business, his father had ordered a large shipment of women's stockings. The stockings were advertised for twenty-five cents a pair and were not selling very vigorously. My great-grandpa, after a few weeks, decided to sell the stockings at a loss.

Not one to take a loss easily, however, my grandfather offered a solution. "Dad," he said, "let me have those stockings. I know we can get twenty-five cents a pair and sell off the whole lot in a week!"

"No way," my great-grandfather insisted. "Let's just forget the stockings and mark them up as a loss."

The next day my grandpa put a sign out in front of the store: *Ladies' Stockings on Sale: 4 Pair for a Dollar.* Women flocked in like june bugs on honey, and by the end of the day, the whole lot had been sold for full price.

My grandpa—the first of the big-time marketing experts!

Some years later, my grandpa expanded his interests and started a trucking business with his brother. They made deliveries, hauled supplies and generally worked from sunrise to sunset.

But before long they had nearly worn themselves to a frazzle with the constant coming and going. After that, my grandpa kept his feet and mind firmly planted in the country store, which increasingly demanded more and more of his time and attention.

When I consider my grandfather and others of his generation, I am reminded of the heritage you and I received from our ancestors. They truly blazed new trails and took great risks.

Today, when we think of our families, it is amazing to realize that there are still new frontiers to explore. Our older generations met every new challenge and embraced every change with a spirit of exploration and resolve to succeed. We owe them much, and their example can teach us to dream just as big.

Many moments and possessions will pass in and out of our lives, but family can be a constant in a world of continual change. A person can buy a house, but not a home. We can buy food and sex and entertainment, but we can't buy warm family conversations, intimacy or quiet evenings on the couch.

I saw this truth firsthand several years ago, when our family had gathered at a local park for a reunion. We were a big clan, large enough that not every face was familiar, not every name known. We began with a blessing over the food, and then everyone followed a line down either side of a row of picnic tables loaded with food.

For the next hour or so, everyone ate and talked, filled and refilled their paper plates until the comfortable fullness of the gut turned to sheer agony. About the time everyone began to moan and groan, a few of us noted one family member who was actually going back for thirds and fourths. He wasn't a big man, rather frail-looking in fact, and he had about him the emaciated frame of a wanderer. Somehow, this family member seemed out of place.

Questions flowed up and down the tables. Do you know that fellow? Did he come with you? No? We thought he came with you! You mean he's not your cousin Virgil? Who is he then? You don't know? We don't know!

Finally, it occurred to everyone that this fellow was no family member at all. Rather, he was a stranger who had been strolling through the park, smelled the good food and decided to make himself a part of the family so he could sample the wares. Most likely this fellow had no family of his own, but that day he was part of us. He not only enjoyed a good meal, but we invited him to participate in the afternoon softball game and the making of homemade ice cream. For all intents and purposes, he became a distant cousin that day.

Being a family is so much more than just living under the same roof. A family consists of people who choose to love each other. Some people, it seems, could only be loved by family. Or, as the old saying goes, some folks are so nasty that only their mothers could love them. But that's what a family is for, isn't it? In a family, even the unlovable are loved.

As I've grown older, I've also become aware that family is where we find those people who accept us, warts and all. Those who love us accept our anger and our pain; they are willing to bear the brunt of our words and our mistakes. Sometimes the people we love the most are the ones we inadvertently hurt the most. We don't mean to, but a husband or wife, a son or daughter, is sometimes the target of our frustration when we have had a bad day at the office or when we are struggling with a stressful situation.

Think about it. How many times have you or I felt frustrated with another person only to bring that frustration home and dump it onto our family? How many times have we been angered by someone at work or by another driver on the way home from work, only to step inside the house and explode in anger toward our spouse or children?

Not long ago I had an unusually bad week. Everyone wanted a chunk of my time, and when I gave them the time, they had some critical word for me. I have never been one to handle negativity well, and I don't do well being around negative people. And so that week, I was inundated by stress.

On Friday, I came home angry at the world. I was short with my children and cross at my wife, and I didn't want to participate in any of the family activities that weekend. Finally, after stewing in my own juices for a while, I realized that I was funneling my anger toward the wrong people. My family had done nothing to bruise me. They loved me. Why was I being cruel and short-tempered toward them?

I know that this scenario occurs in most families, and we should celebrate this kind of sacrificial love. Those who love us well also know us well. A family is where we can find the courage to ask for forgiveness and admit that we have made mistakes. We don't have to be afraid because we know we will be accepted and loved, in spite of our shortcomings and failures.

As far as I am concerned, that is one of the highest achievements of good parenting. When parents are able to admit their mistakes to their children, the family truly blossoms. I know I felt a special bond with my parents when they were able to admit a shortcoming to me or when they admitted that they did not know the answer to a difficult problem. Such honest moments reminded me that my parents needed my help as much as my criticism, and I have wanted to pass this same honesty and vulnerability on to my children. In fact, I always feel a sense of relief when I am able to tell my son or daughter, "I'm sorry. Daddy made a mistake." I even feel empowered when I admit that I am not all-powerful and that I don't have the answers to all of life's problems. Sometimes, as families, we have to struggle through things together. And that is where the real loving begins.

I also believe that family is where we pass along those traditions and beliefs that are important to us. Children naturally respond to and want to believe the same things their parents believe. That is why the home is so important. A parent can teach a child love or hate, prejudice or equality, intolerance or respect—all from our words and attitudes.

A friend of mine has a captivating family tradition that conveys the spirit of love and giving in a dynamic fashion. As a child, he spent his formative years in a government housing project—a small, cramped apartment, which offered little hope or promise for a future. But through hard work, determination and a will to rise above his circumstances, this friend found his way to a new life. However, he has never forgotten those years he spent in the government housing project and the feelings that those circumstances generated.

Now, when Christmas rolls around each year, this friend uses his own history to teach his children the spirit of giving. The family goes shopping together; they buy items that they believe another family might appreciate. They wrap the gifts nicely and then drive across town on Christmas Eve to the same government housing project where my friend grew up. They knock on the same apartment door. And they give the gifts to the family who lives in that apartment—usually a different family each Christmas.

Over the years, they have met with blank stares, suspicious looks and sometimes shrieks of joy from within the apartment. But my friend always makes it a point to tell his story and the reason for the visit: "I lived in this apartment when I was a child. By the grace of God I found a way. You can, too. And here is something to help you celebrate with your family and know the joy of this night. God bless you and merry Christmas."

Sometimes my friend and his family are invited inside. Sometimes they are turned away. But always there is the spirit of love and happiness when my friend and his family return home to celebrate the arrival of the Christ child. Their family tradition of giving has served them well. They are closer because of the traditions they observe together.

All families have observances of one type or another. They may be little traditions like returning to the same vacation spot each summer, or working together to rake the fall leaves, or eating a Thanksgiving meal together; but they give meaning to the word "family," and they help make our days brighter and more meaningful.

This is the blessing of love.

Of all the things we can replace in life, we cannot replace family. We cannot recover lost memories once they are forgotten, and we cannot bring back happy moments once they have passed. In a family, the best we can do is to remake our memories day by day, to love and to support each other in such a way that the goodness remains. Family is where we find our warmth, our center of love. And if we lose that, we have lost a piece of ourselves, I believe.

When I was serving my first parish, I received a phone call one Saturday morning from a lady in distress. She was talking so incoherently, jumping from one phrase to another, that I could scarcely make sense of the conversation. Eventually I figured out who she was and why she was calling. Her name was Margaret, and her house had caught fire in the night and burned to the ground. She was calling from a neighbor's house and wanted me to come right over.

Rushing to the scene, I arrived as the volunteer fire department was dousing the last of the charred rubble. All that remained of her house was the foundation and a heap of smoldering black ash, pungent as landfill waste.

I found Margaret wandering aimlessly through the refuse, seemingly oblivious to the heat that was still rising from the steaming cinders. A fireman called out to her, beckoning her to leave so they could finish hosing off the blackened rubbish. She was oblivious to their cries.

Traipsing into the heap to help her, I realized that Margaret was searching for something. I held her hand, hoping that she might locate the valuable for which she was longing. I urged her to give up the search, but to no avail.

"My living room was about here," she kept saying. "It was right about here."

I dared not ask her what she was looking for—a gold wedding band perhaps, or a diamond necklace? Maybe a lockbox with valuables inside? Perhaps a watch or a string of pearls?

Suddenly Margaret paused, bent and turned over a couple of charred two-by-fours that had served as the walls of her home. There, beneath a clutter of ash, she pulled out a treasure of singed photographs, a small miracle to be sure—pictures in an album that had survived the burning and the dousing. She opened the book slowly and ran her coal-black fingers over the surfaces of the photographs as if she had discovered gold.

"Margaret," I said, "I thought you were looking for valuables."

She turned a page and pointed to a row of brittle photographs. "Here's my wedding picture. And here's a photo of my son and daughter. My grandkids, too!" Every photo seemed to give her great joy. She composed herself, drew in her strength.

"You see," she told me, pointing to the smoldering remnants, "I can replace everything else. But I can't replace these photographs and memories of my family. When you have a tragedy, family is about all that keeps you alive. As long as I've got people who love me, I'll be fine."

I had to agree with her.

Holding hands, Margaret and I walked through the embers toward the yard. The sun was up. The firemen were still working. There was a kind of tranquillity in that moment that was difficult to explain. There was a peace.

Turning around, I was suddenly awed by the sight of a beautiful rainbow arching over the smoldering remains of the house. There, spanning through the firemen's mist and spray, the refracted light of the sun offered a promise to Margaret. She was not forgotten. There would be a tomorrow. Her family and faith would sustain her.

And there would always be a rainbow.

2

Friends

The best mirror is an old friend.

—traditional proverb

To look at them you'd have thought they were six assassins, only sadder, and they were sitting in a row together at the back of the funeral home. I watched these men out of the corner of my eye as I went forward to the casket to greet the widow.

These are the funerals I hate, I said to myself, *when I don't know the family and six hit men show up to serve as pallbearers.*

The widow was nice enough, however. She was in her late forties, attractive, well dressed and sprinkled with gold jewelry. She seemed glad to see me and gave me a hug, thanking me for agreeing to do the funeral service for her husband. I said I was glad to help, sauntered around the flowers for a short time and then waited for further instructions.

At last, when there was a break in the receiving line, the widow turned to me and pointed to the six men at the back. "Why don't you go meet Gilley's friends," she suggested. "They'll have some interesting stories to tell you."

I made my way toward the assassins, pausing long enough to speak to a few other people and strengthen my nerve. Then I shuffled in front of the six men and thrust out my hand. I introduced myself and told them I was the pastor who was going to be doing Gilley's memorial service.

The six rose in unison, buttoned their coats, greeted me warmly. One or two smiled.

"I understand you have some interesting stories about Gilley," I said, pulling up a chair.

One of the men—a hard, weather-beaten fellow with a ponytail and graying temples—was the first to speak. He introduced himself as Jimbo and proceeded to tell me why the six of them were at the funeral.

"All of us go way back," he said. "We all knew Gilley in high school, and we had some great times together. Played on the football team. Four of us went to Vietnam, although we never served in the same outfits. Frank's come all the way from California for the funeral. Bob lives in Arizona. I've stayed close to home all my life. But we've always kept in touch, gotten together at least once a year to catch up on life and raise hell."

The other five gave a fainthearted laugh, but there was something of pain in their voices. A couple of the fellows wrung their hands, searching for words.

"Gilley was the smartest of us," another fellow continued. "He settled down early, married Janet, made a nice life for himself. He was the one we looked to for advice when we had a problem. Gilley really helped me when I was going through my divorce, that's for sure. He was always thinking of the other guy."

Jimbo flipped his ponytail and told a boyhood story of the time Gilley got bucked off a horse. A couple of the others joined in with recollections of their own: Gilley fumbling the ball at the two-yard line in a high school football game; Gilley and Janet getting stranded at a lodge in Montana when the big snowstorm hit; Gilley jumping up in the bleachers at a basketball game to cheer and cracking his head open on a low beam. They all laughed until they began to feel soothed and smothered by the warmth.

Finally someone was bold enough to mention the unmentionable. "Damn cancer," one of them mumbled. "It's not fair."

Jimbo played with his coat button. "I walked for miles in Vietnam and never caught a bullet," he said. "Gilley lives a quiet life, has a wonderful family and is the first to go. I don't understand it."

They all shook their heads in disbelief.

A few minutes later, the funeral director tapped me on the shoulder, and I went up front to deliver the message. I talked about the kind of man Gilley was (although I never knew him), and the kind of husband and father Gilley longed to be. I said all the usual things, and a few things that were unusual, and a great deal I knew nothing about. It seemed there was nothing left to say, and I was about to sit down; but then I remembered the words one of the fellows had offered, and they seemed appropriate.

"Gilley was a good friend," I said. "And most of all he wants to be remembered for good, for joy, for laughter." Briefly I told a few of the stories of friendship that the men had shared with me moments before. At last everyone nodded and smiled, even his wife and children. As a final word, I summarized the theology of the moment with the simple words, "Life is good. Life is beautiful. Life is a gift of God. But it is not fair."

Gilley had come home.

Following the funeral service, I watched as the six men rose and carried the casket to the waiting hearse. At the cemetery, they carried their dear friend to his resting place with pride and dignity, the sun gleaming on their faces, the wind whipping their hair. And after the benediction, they gathered in a circle and wept together—strong men, all—but each diminished by the loss of a friend.

John Donne once wrote, "No man is an island." Oh, we may think that we can walk through life alone, can go it alone, doing our own thing, but somewhere there is a friend who helped make us what we are. Friends are strength; they lend support and hope. What would life be without them?

Some say that old friends are the best friends. This may be true. Although I must attest that I have found deep friendships at every stage of my life.

However, I believe it is accurate that our deepest memories are often attached to those friends who were our childhood companions. Our oldest memories somehow attach themselves to our psyches in such a way that we often see the faces of old friends and remembered times popping up in our dreams, dissolving into beautiful sunsets, merging with the cream in our coffee.

Growing up in a small town, I knew many people by name and face. But I also had good friends. And best friends. When I think of my childhood and adolescence, these are the faces I see.

My first day in the second grade I recall looking around the room for a friendly face. My family had moved to town over the summer, and I knew no one at the beginning of school. But that first day at recess, I met Bryan, and from that day on we were like brothers.

I can't begin to relate all the things that Bryan and I did together, but I know I would be someone else completely if not for his friendship. We played basketball together by the hours, drove the teachers mad and played chess (although he was far better at the game than I). There were days we got into trouble (most every day probably), and we were called into the principal's office together on a few occasions. But by and large, we did fine. I mean, look at the way we turned out!

We even discovered women together. We were probably in the fourth or fifth grade when Bryan found half a pack of naked-lady playing cards lying on the sidewalk. For days we traded the cards back and forth, showed them to the other boys (which made us cult heroes and the envy of every boy in our class), and somehow managed to keep the cards hidden from our parents and teachers. I don't recall what happened to those cards (or do I still carry one in my wallet?), but those were some exciting times.

Somehow I managed to ride Bryan's coattails through school, where he finished at the top of the class. I don't like to think about where I ranked in the academic scheme of things, but even back then I knew I would end up doing something with words—using them to make people think or cry or laugh. I just didn't know how I would pull it off.

Bryan and I are still good friends, although we don't keep in touch as much as we should, family and work obligations and all. But we always have a good time when we get together.

When I was ten years old, my family moved across town to a new house. That was when I met Robin. He was a couple of grades ahead of me, but because of the proximity of our homes, we saw each other almost every day. Robin was something of an outdoorsman, and we often fished together on summer afternoons or played whiffle ball in the field behind our house. We had walkie-talkies and at night, when everyone else was asleep, we turned them on and talked to each other from the sanctuary of our bedrooms. Sometimes we camped out and stayed up half the night, talking about sports and hunting and movies we had seen.

One of our favorite activities was building bicycle ramps. We loved to see how high and far we could fly through the air. These antics were much fun until the day Robin flew a little too high and a bit too far, and nearly broke his collarbone. That kind of put a damper on that activity.

I can't begin to name all the other friends who passed in and out of my life during those early years, but those friendships changed me forever. I still see their faces, and I can recall their names. Some of them are no longer living; others have passed out of my life completely. But they are still a part of me.

I suppose that life itself dictates, to a great degree, who our friends will be. Had I lived in a different town, attended a different school or made other decisions at strategic times, I could have ended up with an entirely different set of friends and memories. But I know I would not be the same person I am today. People touch other people in unique and unalterable ways. Friends change the very fabric of life. There's no denying this.

When I was in graduate school, I spent my first year in a kind of exalted dormitory. By the sheer luck of the draw, I happened to room with a fellow from Beijing, China, named Xiangming. During my grad school years, he was the closest friend I had. He taught me much about life, showed me how to cook authentic Chinese food and gave me a new view of humanity. I helped him learn how to drive, read his research papers, gave him tips on the English language, and helped him to experience American culture and holidays. I could never beat him at table tennis (Ping-Pong), however.

Had Xiangming and I not found our way to the same university and had we not been placed together in that graduate housing by the luck of the draw, I doubt we would have ever met. I know we would never have ended up friends. It kind of makes me wonder from time to time whether life doesn't have some kind of design to it—that things turn out the way they do because certain friendships are meant to happen and certain people are meant to enter our lives at certain times. I don't know. But I'm sure I would be someone less than I am today had I not met Xiangming.

Friendship is a necessary blessing of life because good friends keep us humble. Friends serve as a reminder that the universe does not revolve around any one of us and our petty problems. Friends are people like you and me who have the same concerns, the same values, the same ups and downs. We are all struggling together through this thing called life. We do not pass through life alone.

Friends are those who know how to cry with us and when to laugh until it hurts. And sometimes a friend is someone who reaches out for a little support. We might even have friends we have never met.

I do.

A few years back, I had written some curriculum for teenagers. It was the kind of mumbo-jumbo that most kids would naturally have tossed in the trash. You know, a-middle-aged-man-telling-you-how-to-find-happiness kind of curriculum. I expected to see the stuff in print, but I never imagined that any teenager would actually read it or be affected by it.

That is, until I received a peculiar-looking letter in the mail one day. The envelope was postmarked in South Carolina, and a message had been stamped on the back in black ink: "Inmate Correspondence." I paused before opening the letter. South Carolina? Prison? Whom did I know who was an inmate? Why would someone in prison be writing to me?

I ripped open the envelope and found my answer. A hand-written letter began:

Dear Sir,

You do not know me, but my name is Corey. I am fifteen years old and I am serving some time in the juvenile prison of South Carolina. You probably wonder why I am writing to you.

A couple of weeks ago I was feeling down and went to talk to the chaplain here. He is a nice guy and he helped me a lot. He also gave me some little books to read that talked about how to find happiness in life. I thought it was really good stuff, and it helped me. When I finished reading it, I noticed you were the writer, and that's why I'm writing you.

*Have you written any other stuff? You write neat stuff. If so,
I would like to read it. I also enjoy reading westerns, horror stories and mysteries. Have you written any stuff like that?*

*Please write me back. I don't get many letters here. It gets
kind of lonely sometimes. The chaplain is a nice guy, but he isn't
around all the time. If you write me back, please send some
stamps. If you do, I promise to write you back and tell you more
about myself.*

As soon as I read the letter, I knew I had found a pen
pal. Quickly, I boxed up some books, the kind Corey liked
to read—mysteries, horror stories and westerns—and I
mailed them to him along with a string of stamps. He
wrote me back, and we have been corresponding regularly
ever since.

Although I have never met him, I get the feeling that
Corey is trying very hard to overcome the obstacles in his life.
He writes of his loves and his struggles. He tells me why he
gets sent to detention and admits when he has made a mistake. He is working on getting his high school diploma, and
he wants to go to college. I think he will make it.

There is something simple and elementary about having a
pen pal. Perhaps it reminds me of childhood—when the great
problems of life could be solved with a sugar note and SWAK
(Sealed With A Kiss). A pen pal is wonderful because this
friendship requires little more than the ability to put our feelings on paper and lick a stamp. We all need somebody to
write to. And we could all do with a few more pen pals. I
hope for others. Having a pen pal reminds me that I can hang
on to a bit of my childhood.

These types of early friendships—the kind children share—are often so genuine we adults can scarcely comprehend their purity. Kids have much to teach us about the true nature of friendship.

Every day, all around the world, there are children who like each other, who talk to each other, who get along—all for the sake of friendship. These friendships cut across the racial, religious and social barriers we adults have erected. But kids are kids. They are not concerned about such things. To a child, a friend is someone who will sit at the opposite end of the teeter-totter.

Perhaps you've heard the one about the little boy who came home late for supper. His mother asked, "Why are you late, Johnny?"

"Because," Johnny explained, "I saw another little boy sitting beside the road. His bike was busted. So I helped him fix things up."

"But you don't know anything about fixing a bicycle," his father said.

"I know," Johnny admitted. "But I sat down on the road next to him. I listened. We had a good cry. And then I gave him a ride home."

Children know that friendship has a great deal more to do with empathy and presence than usefulness and appearance. They want someone to hang on to. They want a shoulder to cry on.

Several years ago, when I visited Israel, I read about two girls on the West Bank near Jerusalem who had created an unusual friendship. They played together, did all the usual little girl stuff, like dressing dolls, playing house and creating pretend games. *So what?* you may ask. *What's the big deal?*

No big deal, except one of the girls is Jewish and the other is Muslim. Somehow, despite the great historical and religious adversities of that region, they had managed to find each other and form a friendship on the West Bank. The author who wrote the story pointed out that this friendship had blossomed despite the overwhelming odds against it—a tiny miracle of love in an ocean of hate. And if two little girls can make a friendship . . . well, maybe there is hope for the world after all.

Children seem to form friendships quickly. They love and give without reservation. They are more spontaneous and free than most adults.

However, some people get to be good friends in a short period of time. They hit it off because they have common experiences, or have gone through difficult times, or share a love of the same beer. Some folks even have more friends than they know what to do with. I envy them.

Take my friend Jane, for instance. She and her husband were the first to build a house on a new cul-de-sac. As other homes were built and the families moved in, she was the first to greet them. She bathed them in gifts and goodies: home-made candies, neighborhood brochures, invitations to come to a cookout at her house. Before long, she was friends with everyone on both sides of the road.

She organized block parties and summer gatherings, and even went to the trouble of watching other people's children when they had to run to the grocery store for a gallon of milk. I don't think there was a person within a mile of her home who didn't know Jane. She was that kind of person.

When I talk with people about friendship, it seems that most of us believe we have enough friends, but few very close friends. I wonder why.

Perhaps it is because we are conditioned as we grow older to hold so much of ourselves back. We allow few people to know the core of our being, where our heart is. We don't talk much about our problems, and when we do, we often pay other people to listen to us.

In the movie *Crocodile Dundee*, there is a revealing scene where Dundee is talking with some fellows in a bar. One guy tells Dundee that a friend of his is going to see a shrink. Dundee, from the Australian outback, doesn't understand what the fellow is talking about.

"You know . . . a shrink," the fellow explains. "A psychiatrist. A person who listens to other people's problems."

"What's the matter?" Dundee wants to know. "Don't he have any mates [friends]?"

Nothing against psychiatrists and counselors, but I think that movie hit upon something. People who feel lonely or stressed may have a deeper need for friendship than anything else. Perhaps, in our fast-paced lifestyle and looking-out-for-number-one kind of philosophy, we have missed the obvious: We need friends. Getting to the top may have its rewards, but what is to be gained by loneliness?

This truth came home to me a few years ago when a young woman walked into my office. She was immaculately dressed, successful-looking, seemed to have everything going for her. I had seen her picture in the newspaper every week and recognized that she was one of the top-selling real estate brokers in the area. She drove a nice car, owned a large, beautiful home and seemed to be living the good life. I couldn't imagine her having any problems or worries at all.

But after a few minutes, it became apparent that she was a most unhappy and unfulfilled individual. Through a cascade of tears, she told me about her broken marriage and the huge debt she had assumed to feed her growing image of success. Mostly she spoke of her loneliness. She was in such despair she was considering packing up her belongings, moving to another city and beginning a whole new life.

I suggested that she get together with some of her family and friends to talk about these matters openly and honestly, asking for their help. But she seemed perplexed, even insulted, by this suggestion.

"I'm alienated from my family, and I don't *have* friends," she said. "There's just *me*."

The more we talked, the more I realized that this woman didn't have friends because she didn't know how to *be* a friend. Over the years, she had probably stepped on, jilted, backstabbed and tossed aside every person who got in the way of her ultimate self-fulfilling goals. Now she had come to the end of her rope, and there was no one there to help her. And who would want to? No one wants to be used.

When she finally left the office, I felt like a rich man. When it comes to friends, I always have.

A final account of friendship. True story.

In the summer of 1983, I drove into the heart of the Pisgah national forest near Asheville, North Carolina, to serve a small church in the mountains. Initially, I must confess that I expected to encounter folks there who more closely resembled

Jed Clampett and Granny than any damn Yankee like myself. I could not have been more wrong. The folks I met in that mountain haven were sophisticated, warm and loving. They welcomed me with open arms, and I quickly made some good friends.

The beauty of their mountain town was breathtaking. On Sunday mornings, I could gaze into the valley behind the church and see the majestic Biltmore House nestled in the distance. Tree-covered peaks rose all around. The air seemed fresher than any I had ever breathed.

That summer I participated in many events with the teenagers and learned the arts of tubing (swimming downstream reclining in an inner tube) and mountain climbing. Most of those teenagers were in great condition. All those years in the mountains had made them hard and tough. They really enjoyed life, and many of their activities were physically demanding. Most everyone was able to participate.

Everyone, that is, except Susie, a younger teen who had been born with a degenerative muscular disease. From her birth she had been forced to wear a set of steel braces, which ran up the sides of her legs and joined together around her hips. On most of the youth outings, she was able to go as far as the first trail or to the drop-off point, and then her parents had to take her back home. Everyone in the group knew this wasn't fair, and we searched desperately for ways to include Susie in the activities.

One morning, during my last week with the teenagers, the kids decided to celebrate my departure by climbing Mount Pisgah—the third highest peak in the Smoky Mountains—and one of the favorite places they had shown me that summer. We were all excited about the hike, and we were blessed with an unusually clear day.

As usual, Susie and her parents showed up to wish me goodbye. They did not have to drive very far. In fact, Susie lived in a house on the side of Mount Pisgah, in the shadow of the peak that others had talked about over the years, but whose summit she had never seen. All of her life, she had heard others talk about Mount Pisgah, what it was like to journey to the top, what it was like to look down upon the world and view the beauty and splendor of that land. But she had never seen it.

However, that day was different.

As we were about to leave, one of the teenagers blurted out what everyone was thinking and hoping. "Susie, you come with us!" she insisted. "We'll get you to the top."

Susie's mother gasped. I could see the concern in her eyes. She had been to the top and knew that Pisgah was tough going, especially the last half mile.

"Can I, Mama?" Susie asked her mother.

"Honey, I don't think you'd better. It's too steep. You could get hurt."

"We'll take turns carrying her," one of the boys in the youth group suggested. "We'll get her to the top together."

Her mother seemed unmoved by the idea, but Susie was unrelenting. "Let me, Mama. Let me go. I want to see what's up there."

At last her mother gave in and let her little girl go. She stooped down and removed the steel braces from the sides of Susie's legs. One of the strongest guys in the youth group, a big, strapping high school senior who played on the football team, gathered Susie into his arms and began carrying her up the trail.

The first mile or so seemed easy as we took turns carrying Susie, sometimes doubling up when we came to a more demanding slope. Susie could scarcely contain her mounting excitement. "How much farther?" she kept asking like an anxious child. "How close are we to the top?"

We proceeded up the trail to the final stage before the summit push—a slope of rock steps and adjoining plateaus that appeared to go straight into the heavens. Everyone paused to regain their breath before the ascent, but Susie seemed lighter than ever. Taking turns every few feet, we shifted Susie back and forth on our backs, climbing by stages, until we reached the summit.

As Susie's friends stepped out of the shadows of the trees into the glorious sunlight, they began to shout. Susie danced from shoulder to shoulder as everyone celebrated the achievement.

That day was beyond belief. The sun was stretched out behind a line of huge white clouds, their shadows floating over a sea of velvet green. Birds flew below us, giving the impression that we, too, could fly. When the clouds parted momentarily, a long ray of sunlight streamed into the valley, and we could see for miles.

As we stood there with Susie, friends every one, there were shouts of joy and tears of triumph. For the first time in her life, Susie no longer had to look up at the mountain. Now she was looking down, with the whole world at her feet. Far below, nestled on the mountainside like a patch of brown fabric, was Susie's house.

That day, on a mountain called Pisgah, I recalled that it was from a peak bearing the same name that Moses looked

out across the Promised Land and wept for joy and the longing of home. I suppose that is how we felt when we arrived at
that promised land of friendship and knew nothing could
take that moment away from Susie.

Months passed. It was some time later that I received a
card from Susie's mother, a kind of Christmas greeting that
had traveled across several states to find me among the bar-
ren cornfields of Indiana beside a crackling winter fire.

"You'll never know what it meant to Susie to climb that
mountain last summer," her mother wrote. "All of her life she
had watched her friends leave for the top, only to be turned
back by her disability. But when she made it to the top . . .
well, it changed her life. She still talks about it. She talks
about those friends who made it possible. And someday, she
knows she'll get to the top again."

Along the journey of our lives, each of us knows the power
of friendship. There are times when friends carry us along
through moments or days of despair and heartache. And there
are times when being a friend means bearing the load for someone else. But regardless, a friend is someone who is willing to
make the journey, who is willing to go to the top or descend
into the abyss. A friend is someone on whom we can depend.

Whether you and I have few friends or more than we can
count, the blessing of friendship remains the same. We are
put here on this earth for relationship, to learn the lessons of
love and community. Having friends, and being a friend, is
what makes life fun and adventurous.

Friends are the trusted treasures of life. Squander them,
and you end up in poverty. Imagine a life without friendship,

and you pine for friendship all the more. Consider the prospect of parting with a friend forever, and you feel a sudden sadness.

I know. In my desk I keep a reminder of one parting. They are words that were given to me before a friend moved away and left me with little more than snapshots and memories. Before leaving, however, he entrusted to me this Gaelic blessing of friendship. These words could be a sign of blessing to all friends everywhere:

> *May there always be work for your hands to do.*
> *May your purse always hold a coin or two.*
> *May the sun always shine warm on your windowpane.*
> *May a rainbow be certain to follow each rain.*
> *May the hand of a friend always be near you.*
> *And may God fill your heart with gladness to cheer you.*

3

Children

Children and fools cannot lie.

—John Heywood

The notion that children are *free* may seem a contradiction to many people. After all, children begin to drain our bank accounts from the moment of birth, and the siphoning doesn't stop until after they have graduated from college, found a job or moved out of the house at the age of thirty-seven. Yet children are, without doubt, one of the greatest blessings of life and the highest source of joy on earth—beautiful miracles we can never truly own or possess.

Thank God I learned this lesson in the early stages of my parenting. I have never recoiled from the realization that I do not own my children. I can love them, teach them, lead them, discipline them, hold them, scold them, mold them, show them, support them, believe in them and embrace them

. . . but I always have to let them go. They are as free as I believe myself to be. They are *my* children, but they belong to the wind, and the trees, and the flowers, and the stars, and all the stuff of life; and, in the end, they will go where they want to go, and do what they want to do, and be what they want to be. I can never mold them into someone they are not. I cannot make them think certain thoughts or have certain feelings. I cannot keep them. They belong to the One who made them, and that is all right with me.

Being a parent, however, is without doubt the craziest occupation ever invented. No one who is, or has ever been, a parent can deny the fact that parenting requires far more energy than any individual has to give. Parenting requires patience and stamina and wisdom and a degree of self-confidence unlike that required in any other walk of life.

Living with children is akin to enjoying a twenty-four-hour root canal. But living in a world without children would be far more excruciating. What person, even if not a parent, could imagine a world without little faces, sticky fingers and bright eyes filled with wonder?

Parenting is a round-the-clock affair. Being a parent is a type of on-the-job training. There are no college courses or degrees given. But somehow most parents manage to become experts in a short period of time. What amazes me is that so many people actually survive this onslaught and live to tell about it.

As I look back on my own childhood, I am convinced that, secretly, my parents must have beaten their heads against the wall each night, taken huge loads of aspirin and cried themselves to sleep on many occasions. When I was ten or eleven years old, I accidentally shot a hole in the windshield of my parents' new car with my BB gun. Once, when I was old enough to push a lawnmower, I forgot about the new air conditioner my dad had installed at the side of the house, and I nonchalantly proceeded to mow the electrical cable into a mass of frayed wires. That was a hotter summer than usual.

My first driving experience occurred when I was fourteen. My father and I were working in a small field adjacent to our house. As it was getting along toward supper time, he handed me the keys to the El Camino and said, "You might as well practice working that clutch. Drive that sucker up to the house and park it in the carport next to the Buick." His confidence inflated my pubescent ego to the point of no return, and when the steely keys hit my palm and I heard the rattle of the engine and saw the first puff of exhaust fumes emanating from the rusted tail pipe, I knew I was a man.

I chucked the gear shift into reverse, popped the clutch and shot backward like a bat out of hell before the engine died, some twenty feet away. My father was still smiling, so I cranked on the ignition until I caught a spark, jammed the El Camino into first gear and began to move, in herky-jerky fashion, across the field toward the road. I managed to kill the engine a dozen times before reaching that sacred patch of asphalt we called a street, but by then I'd gotten the hang of it and was feeling quite comfortable in my new role as driver.

I looked both ways, pulled out onto the road, and drove slowly past the neighbors' houses, waving to friends, fiddling with the radio and other assorted knobs, and occasionally leaning out the window to spit. At last I came to our driveway.

As I inched the car onto the gravel and headed toward the carport, however, I began to feel the first twinges of my mortality. The path leading to the carport looked surprisingly narrow, and a wooden fence loomed closer with each passing inch. Funny how I had never noted these things when my father was behind the wheel.

Rounding the turn leading up to the carport, I felt my right foot slip off the brake at the exact moment that all sense of time and space left my body and my vision began to blur. What happened next is still a black hole in my memory. I was jabbing wildly at the clutch and brake while rounding the turn. The world turned upside down. Things happened. The horizon spun.

Somehow I managed to miss the fence with the front bumper as I simultaneously aimed at the vacant slot next to the Buick. I found the brake again as I eased the El Camino into the carport accompanied by the teeth-gritting squeal of metal grinding against metal. When the car stopped, I knew my odyssey was over (and, most likely, my life).

Out of the tall grasses of the back field, I saw my father running toward the house. When he came within earshot, I heard him yell, "What happened? What have you done?"

I didn't answer right away since my sense of equilibrium was still returning and I had no idea what had happened. I pulled the keys out of the ignition, slid out of the car (noting there was more space than usual between the wall of the carport and the driver's side) and walked around to review the damage done to the Buick. My father arrived, out of breath and sweating, and casually remarked that I had sideswiped the Buick. The cars were parked so close together a dime would not have fit between them!

How my father backed the El Camino out of that predicament without inflicting damage I will never know. But I can attest that, in spite of the sharp grinding sound that had shivered down the entire length of the chassis, there was not one fleck of paint missing from the finish of either car. My dad laughed about my driving effort for days afterward, even to the point of embarrassing me with his goodness. This driving experience is one of the primary reasons I believe in letting children learn from their mistakes. It was the first time in my life I knew conclusively that there was a God.

I know that I have all of this, and more, to look forward to with my own young children. And I can't wait.

Over the years, I have learned so much from children. Not just my own, but even from those I meet on the street or at the mall.

One day I was at a local park and happened to see a little boy picking up the aluminum pop cans littering the landscape. I went over and commended him for helping to save the environment. "Oh, I'm not doing this for the environment, mister," he told me. "My big brother and his friends are over there on the basketball court, but they won't let me play. So I'm collecting cans. When I get enough cans, I'm going to cash them in. Then I'm going to buy my own basketball. And when I get that new ball, you can bet they'll be asking me to play!"

I didn't know whether to believe this boy would grow up to be a successful entrepreneur or a master at the art of bribery, but he sure impressed me with his savvy. No doubt he could teach a few of us adults a thing or two about sticking with it, not giving up and finding an innovative solution to a vexing problem. I'm certain that kid will make a fine parent someday.

Another time, I overheard two little girls talking in the mall. Evidently the subject was boys, as they were extolling the virtues of their fair sex and the inferiority of the male anatomy . . . or what they knew of it. "That's Jimmy Quigins," one little girl said. "He can't even do the splits at recess."

"You know why, don't you?" the other asked, giggling.

"Why?"

"Because he's got that thing on his body."

"Oh, yeah," the first little girl said matter-of-factly. "My brother's got it, too."

Children have a way of saying the unsayable, of making complex dilemmas seem simplistic. They are able to make us laugh when we feel like crying, and they give us hope for a better tomorrow.

Some years ago, when I was a chaplain at a large research hospital in North Carolina, I would visit the burn center to check on the children who were recovering there. These were some of the most difficult visits I ever made—seeing the tiny hands and feet wrapped in gauze, trying to look away from the watery eyes that peered at me from beneath layers of sterile cloth. But even though these moments were painful, they were also helpful to me, for I learned that the strength of the human spirit begins with children and, if anything, may actually weaken as we grow older.

Most often, in spite of their difficulties and horrible injuries, the children in the burn center were able to laugh and play as children do. Some did not even seem to realize they were burned. They just wanted to go home. They wanted to be with their family and friends. They wanted to be in school.

One of the chaplains who was on staff there—and a burn victim himself—summarized his feelings about these children at a seminar for families and friends of burn victims. He told them, "When you are with your child, demonstrate your own courage and conviction that healing will take place. Give your children this strength, and they will give it back to you tenfold. I can say without fear of contradiction that over the years I have seen these children give back far more love and encouragement than they have inside. Children heal. But more important than that, they heal us."

Children, I'm convinced, do give us far more than we adults deserve. Society does not often recognize the situation of children. After all, kids can't speak for themselves. They can't have their own radio or television talk shows, or publish their own books. And most of the time, we look right over them when we are mingling at a party or greeting a group of people. Rarely do we stoop to shake hands with a child. And often their needs come last in a long line of personal wants and goals.

Since our society is so competitive and driven, it is often easy for parents to live their lives vicariously through their children. It seems that some parents unknowingly push their children to succeed at sports or academics in the hope that the accolades the child receives will somehow elevate the parent. This was never more real to me than during my college years, when I used to referee grade school basketball games in my native Hoosier state of Indiana.

To the rest of the nation, it may appear that basketball is a sport. But in Indiana, basketball is a religion, and the people who play it and watch it often approach the court with the intensity of pit bulls. Walking onto the court as a referee under these conditions requires not only a master's knowledge of the game, but also an ironclad resolve to persevere under hardship and to survive the barrage of verbal attacks you are bound to receive from people who would, under normal circumstances, be friends and neighbors.

It was in this arena that I first observed the joy of children at play and the utter torment of the parents who watched them. In one highly memorable game, three nine-year-old boys collided with each other near midcourt on the opening tip-off. Blood flowed, I called fouls, and both coaches began screaming like baboons. Parents, faces red with perspiration and anger, screamed at me for justice. One fellow lunged at me with a clenched fist. The children were carried to the locker room, however, proud of their battle scars and none the worse for wear.

After a time-out, play continued. More fouls. Lots of double-dribbles. A turnover every thirty seconds. The game clock ticked away with the speed of molasses. Finally the first quarter was over. Only three more periods to go.

As I continued to referee these little boys, however, a strange thing happened. I began to see these children as children, not as accomplished athletes. For the first time in my illustrious refereeing career, these kids were hilarious to watch. I relaxed. I was cracking up, laughing right into my whistle. Other people were laughing, too. I could see the restrained smiles of parents and coaches.

Before the beginning of the second half, I grew bold and asked both coaches to meet me at center court. "I'm not going to call traveling, double-dribble or three seconds in the lane,"

I told them. "Let's just see if the kids can have some fun."

I was amazed that the coaches agreed with me. In fact, I think they were rather relieved. After all, how do you coach a team that makes two hundred turnovers in a half?

The rest of the game was pure joy. Parents clapped for baskets made by the opposing team. The coaches never stirred on the bench. A few people even got into the spirit of the game and started watching the little cheerleaders who were trying desperately to do handstands and back-flips. I called few fouls or violations that second half. And, best of all, every single boy got to play in the game. Somehow, winning or losing wasn't the primary concern that day. I think everyone had a much better time of it, even the boys themselves.

Children are not meant to bring us pain. They are born to give us joy. And we would all be a lot better off if we took a time-out from our own agendas to give attention to what is truly important to our children. I've never believed that children want to compete with each other—that's an adult agenda that comes later in life. What children want is each other. They crave imagination, and discovery, and laughter itself. They just want to be out there on the playground, or the field, or the court, knowing that they are the center of attention, that we care about them rather than their accomplishments.

Children don't ask for much. They just want to be loved. And love is free.

Long ago a wise person wrote some beautiful words in the Book of Proverbs: "Grandchildren are the crown of the aged, and the glory of children is their parents." (Prov. 17:6 New Revised Standard Version). How marvelous this wonder is when we grasp it. Children are the jewels of life, the crowning achievement of those who love.

Just being around children has its own rewards. We don't have to have children or grandchildren of our own to know the life-giving joy of childhood. All we have to do is visit a playground, or a classroom, or a soccer field on a Saturday morning, and we will find some of the best smiles and happiest faces anywhere.

One lady I know has made a life of helping children as a crossing guard. Every morning, I meet her as I walk my daughter to school. She is an older lady, rather stodgy and crusty-looking at first glance; but she takes a great deal of pride in her work, and she's always there for the boys and girls, rain or shine. In fact, she relates more easily with the children than with adults.

One day, through a casual conversation, I learned that she had been coming to the school every morning and afternoon for decades. "I've got the longest tenure of any crossing guard in the state!" she told me with pride. I could imagine her helping men and women across the street who had once gone to the school themselves as children, and I realized the entire community would be diminished somehow if it were not for her daily love of children and her commitment to them.

No, children don't ask for much. They just want to know that they are loved.

And perhaps this is why they so often drain us of energy. It is difficult, sometimes, amid the stress of job and traffic and daily demands, to love well. Love is the most demanding work of all. Love requires our time and energy and presence when all we really want to do is fall upon the bed and sleep.

I didn't think I would ever get through the first weeks of infancy with my children. Up every night at a quarter of two, my wife and I took turns rocking our children back to sleep, most often falling asleep ourselves in the process. As a husband, I did this faithfully until I learned the male trick of pretending not to hear the midnight cry. My energy levels rose after that, while my wife seemed to grow more and more weary each day. But I have to admit, she was the better parent. It was her love that got her through the long hours.

Still, I have been forced to endure other nights, other long days, trying vacations, mounds of homework, and practices and recitals. . . . and I would do it all again in a heartbeat for the joy of having children. As children grow into their teen years, parents merely trade one set of concerns and worries for another (or so I've heard). Instead of worrying about scraped knees and bruised egos, parents are forced to deal with the pitfalls of dating and driving. Late-night feedings turn into late nights waiting by the window or by the phone. Children just take us from one phase of worry to another. But they are still our children, no matter how old they are.

Children are also the greatest source of laughter we will ever find in life. Kids just look funny when you think about it. They have big heads and little bodies, and until they grow into their skins they are mighty awkward—and likely to say anything at any time.

Over the years, my wife and I have been embarrassed more than a few times by something our son or daughter has said in public. I suspect we are not alone in this susceptibility to complete emotional annihilation. A few times, I have been on the receiving end of some juicy remark a child has spoken concerning his parents. I must confess that I prefer to hear about other people's private lives than to have my own foibles discussed in a public setting.

On most Sunday mornings, I spend time talking with children in church. These children's moments are, by the admission of many adults, the pinnacle of the worship experience. Never mind my sermon.

Oh the tidbits of gossip I have picked up from children over the years! Some seem to never stop talking, even when I am trying to teach a lesson. I have learned to teach with one side of my brain while listening with the other. And I listen closely to pick up on any family secrets that the children may want to share with the whole world.

Once, when I was in North Carolina serving a couple of rural churches, I was telling the children the gospel story of Jesus turning water into wine. One little boy raised his hand.

"My grandpappy makes wine in the cellar!" he disclosed proudly.

I had never considered the possibility that grandfather might be a moonshiner until I looked back at the old man. Grandpa's face was flushed with embarrassment, and he was slowly sinking in his pew.

On another Sunday, a little girl sidled up next to me and yanked incessantly on my sleeve for several minutes while I tried to talk to the children about the pain, anguish and suffering of being a true Christian. Finally, unable to endure her tugging any longer, I acknowledged the little girl. "There's a bug in my ear," she told me, "and it hurts me."

"Oh?" I asked. "You once had a bug in your ear. Did your mommy get it out?"

"No! It's in there right *now*," she insisted. "I can hear it buzzing!"

I never did learn if mommy got the bug out, but several adults did mention that, although they didn't learn much about Christian suffering from that talk, they did learn more about *my* suffering from that experience.

I also heard of the time a fellow was talking to the children of the congregation about being afraid of the dark. "Do you ever get afraid at night and hear strange sounds?" he asked.

One little girl raised her hand. "When I was smaller, I used to hear sounds coming from my mommy and daddy's bedroom," she said.

Unable to stem the flow of words, the leader could only listen helplessly as the little girl continued down the inevitable path of full disclosure.

"They were sounds like 'uhhhggg,' 'ooohhh,' 'aaahhh.' But now I go to sleep earlier, and I don't hear them anymore. I think it was just the television."

Children, I suppose, were put on this earth to humble the proud and to remind us that we can never take life too seriously. As long as there are children, there will be time for play, time for cookies and ice cream and candy, and there will be bedtime stories that we long to believe in every bit as much as the child.

Children remind us that life is not about being the biggest, the best, the richest or the most powerful. Life is about finding a place for everyone in the sandbox, getting our hands dirty and not worrying about it. It's about make-believe, and believing in others, and going to bed at night good and tired after a long day's play. Life is about getting up the next day, taking a bath and starting all over again, growing as we go.

Before I had children, I had my own theories about child rearing, most of them rather harsh and judgmental. I'd go to a restaurant and see a kid squirting ketchup into the salt shaker, and I'd say, "You know, if that were my kid . . ." I'd watch some child throwing a tantrum at the mall and I'd think, *Why doesn't the parent do something about that kid?*

These were my theories, and every one of them worked. But then I had kids, and all my theories dissolved into nothing the first time I watched my son dump the contents of the Parmesan cheese shaker onto the floor at the fancy Italian restaurant. Now I scour the parenting and child magazines, not for answers, but to confirm my suspicions that other parents are as ignorant as I am. I look first for the articles written by some childless Ph.D. These are always good for a laugh.

Being a good parent has nothing to do with knowing the latest theories on child rearing. Good parents have nerves of steel, carry candy at all times, and know how to use diaper wipes and Kleenex in 101 creative ways. And it never hurts to carry Grandma's phone number, either.

I can always tell the difference between an actual parent and a wanna-be. Parents are the ones who can watch a movie and enjoy it even when their kids are howling like wolves. Wanna-bes are the ones who make faces, move to the other side of the movie theater and whisper, "If that were my kid . . ."

I'm glad I have children to remind me that I'm not as stupid as I seem. I'm glad my kids confirm what I have always suspected: that I can do this parenting gig and get away with it. I've even fooled myself into believing that I'm a pretty good daddy.

My son, who just turned four at the time of this writing, recently came home from nursery school, his lower lip quivering. "What happened?" my wife asked him.

"Someone hurt my feelings," he said.

"What happened? Did another boy push you on the playground? Are you hurt?"

"No. Someone hurt my *feelings*," he said.

"Who?"

"A little girl."

Without a moment's hesitation, I turned to my son and told him the way of the world.

"Get used to it," I said. "The girls will hurt your feelings for the rest of your life."

I was proud of that moment, and I gave myself a gold star that evening. Better yet, I think the kid actually knew what I was talking about.

Children are wise, too. They often have the good sense to steer clear of trouble, and sometimes they can see trouble coming when adults cannot. Perhaps this is because children's minds are not yet cluttered with so many unimportant and trivial affairs. Innately many children seem to know what is vital and what is not. They can separate fiction from reality far more readily than we would like to admit. They know what is most important, and they want to help whenever possible.

Take, for instance, the little boy who came up to me several years ago at an amusement park. I was standing on a high deck overlooking a log flume ride when he approached, tugged on my pant leg and told me, "Mister, if you stand here, you're gonna get soaked!"

"Thanks," I said, brushing him off with my I've-got-everything-under-control attitude.

Seconds later, after the little shaver had vamoosed, I knew I was in big trouble, but could scarcely begin to do anything about it. The boat descended down the flume, hit bottom with a mighty thud and sent a thick wave of water directly over my head, drenching me completely from head to foot.

I shook myself off like a wet dog and heard the cheers from a chorus of adult onlookers standing on an adjacent deck. I felt like a fool as I slogged down the steps, water gushing from my shoes each time I bore down with my weight. At the bottom of the steps, I met the kid, standing there in the brilliant sunshine with his arms crossed, smiling at me. He didn't say a word, but his gaze said, "I told you so."

Wisdom comes in many forms and begins early in life.

My son has managed to find his own unique brand of wisdom. It is called survival of the fittest.

Several months ago, when my wife was working late on a Wednesday night, I was in the kitchen cooking a tasty dinner of Hamburger Helper, canned peas, canned peaches and pickled beets (also canned). My son was in the living room, being very cooperative—and very quiet. In fact, after a time, I realized he was being *too* quiet.

I left the stove for a moment and peeked around the corner to see what he was up to. There, sitting on the fancy living room rug, I saw my son working on his latest piece of art. He had found a set of black markers and was energetically drawing rainbows on pieces of paper. The only problem was, each time he began and ended a rainbow, the markers moved off the paper and onto the fancy rug, leaving arching black lines that were beginning to form a nice pattern. By the looks of things, he had been at it a long time.

Naturally, being the good father that I am, I responded to my son in the same fashion my father had responded to me, and his father before him, in such situations: I screamed! "What are you doing?!" I yelled. "What . . . what . . . aaaggghhh!"

Thinking quickly, however, I passed off the problem to Mommy. "When Mommy gets home, she is going to skin you alive!" I yelled.

My son, sensing, somehow, that I was upset, ran into his bedroom, crying and wailing every step of the way. I let him go, hoping that a good cry would do us both some good.

I went back into the kitchen and finished the dinner. A few minutes later, my son came out of his room and climbed into my lap, looking up at me with his big, watery eyes.

"I don't want you to be mad at me, Daddy," he said, sniffling.

I tried to explain the situation and bring some manner of teaching and forgiveness to bear on the outcome.

"Do you know what Mommy is going to do when she comes home and sees what you've done to her rug?"

My son's eyes widened. What was it I had said earlier? He wasn't sure what to make of his predicament. "Mommy's going to skin me alive," he whispered sheepishly, conjuring up images I could scarcely imagine.

"We can do one of two things," I told my son. "When Mommy gets home, you can tell her what you've done, or I can tell her. Which is it going to be?"

My son pondered the choices for a moment, glanced back at his artwork on the rug and swallowed hard.

"Do you want to tell Mommy what you've done? Or do you want Daddy to tell her?" I repeated.

Finally my son offered his option: "I want Daddy to clean it up before Mommy gets home."

Yes, children have an uncanny knack for knowing how to survive and thrive. They can make even the most bizarre situations seem trivial. They can melt our anger with their own brand of logic and simple faith. A world without children would prove to be a bland, sterile existence: no peanut butter and jelly sandwiches, no nursery rhymes, no broken toys to fix, no clothes to mend or scraped knees to bandage. I would venture to say that all of these simple joys and catastrophes would be missed, even yearned for, in their absence.

Often the greatest blessings we enjoy are the ones we experience, and sometimes curse, in the daily, mundane arenas of life. These are the blessings we see each day but rarely stop to ponder and appreciate.

I have heard many parents lament the passing of their children's innocence on numerous occasions. The simple days of childhood seem to pass quickly, leaving parents with full-grown adolescents, fading memories and yellowing photographs of children who have grown up far too fast.

The passing of childhood leaves us, perhaps, waking in the shadows of our own mortality, an awareness that we are growing older and that, as much as we would like to, we cannot stop time's rapid march. Not even our own children will stop to wait for us. They have their own lives to live, their own futures to claim. One day they will leave behind the teddy bear and the rag doll, forsake the playhouse and the family table to begin a life of their own.

As much as we would like to keep our children, we know that, when the last dinner bell rings and we have packed the stuffed animals in the U-Haul and they are headed for the college dorm, we finally have to let them go. But perhaps this is the greatest blessing of all: to know and understand that we have done all that we could, that we did our level best to be good and loving parents. No matter how far our children may travel from home, or how long they stay away, we know they will always remain what they are in our hearts: our children. And, someday, any day, when they come home again, we know there will always be a place at the table, a full glass and an easy chair next to the fireplace with their name on it.

Children may cost us money from time to time, but they are free. They don't take; they give. And they keep on giving in those silent places of the heart.

Most often, when I am with my daughter (whom other people say looks exactly like her daddy), I tend to see her in the light of a lifetime rather than a moment. I see her as a little girl who loves to play with dolls, read books and invent imaginary games for her own entertainment. I try to see the woman she is going to become. She is my daughter, and I love her.

But there are other moments, rare in number, when another kind of love passes between us and, in looking into her eyes, I see not only the little girl that she is, but also myself. She is a part of me. I am in her; she is in me.

It is clearer to me in that moment than in any other that when I am looking into her face, I am not just gazing into the eyes of my child: I am also seeing the face of God.

PART TWO

....

The Greatest of These

4

Faith

Faith is the assurance of things hoped for,
the conviction of things not seen.

—Heb. 11:1 NRSV

Not long ago, when I was feeling down, I took a walk through our church's day-care center. Peeking into the rooms, I was greeted with the sights and sounds of children at play—a group of active boys building a ship out of wooden blocks, a teacher showing a little girl how to tie her shoe, another group of children who had gathered in a corner to dabble in finger painting. In one room, the children had circled the table for their snack and were saying a joyful prayer. From another room I heard the happy strains of the song "Jesus Loves Me."

I returned to my office that day with a spring in my step, certain that I had witnessed moments of faith—little paint-speckled faces and hands curious with creativity, tiny voices opening in prayer, hearts filled with song, minds eager to embrace, to love, to grow. And I wondered—*If this isn't faith, what is?*

Jesus once said, "If you want to know what faith is all about, just watch a child." Or something like that. Better yet, don't grow up too fast. Best to stay childlike as long as possible. You might miss something if you begin thinking like an adult.

Well, I'm not exactly certain what Jesus meant by this, but I have an idea. I have a feeling that faith bears a closer resemblance to giggling than to praying. I have an idea that faith has more to do with Play-Doh and painting than singing from hymnals and reciting tired words. I have the notion that faith is more like making a game out of life than going through life playing games.

My own experience bears this out. As a pastor, every week I meet folks who are unusually bored by the stuff that commonly passes as worship, and I find, as I get older, that I want so much more out of life and faith than I can ever seem to find in any institutionalized religion. I wish I could get back to having fun again. I think that's where God wants to take me . . . and you.

Some years ago I worked with a group of teenagers who were planning a Sunday morning worship service. They had spent time studying the teachings of Jesus and had determined that Jesus was no killjoy. He loved to have fun. They found that many of the parables of Jesus talked about banquets and parties and big, blowout bashes. They determined that Jesus loved wine and song, and enjoyed his friends. They reasoned that faith had more to do with reveling in the grace of God and the goodness of life than in sticking to the rules and playing it safe.

One afternoon, the teenagers stood in the center of the church and thought of all the ways they could have some real fun with their faith. They imagined balloons and streamers, brightly colored banners, birthday music and candles. They imagined flowers and finger paintings and the sound of people singing new tunes. They imagined play mats and straw hats and even dogs and cats. And it wasn't even Christmas.

They thought about all the ways they could make things brighter and louder and richer and higher. They tried to imagine surprises and bow-covered packages and love letters. They thought of ways to make faith fun or cheerful or bursting with color.

It all seemed so simple.

But eventually they came to their senses when a few of the adults complained. What if someone didn't want to have fun in a worship service? What if some folks were offended by party streamers and balloons and all this talk of God's grace?

Why, most folks had learned to count on their faith just the way it is. They didn't want change. They didn't like for anyone to tinker with sacred rituals. They'd grown to count on their faith as something immutable and . . . well, serious. And in a serious faith, there is no room for streamers and poppers and balloons and finger painting. No room for laughing and joking and making funny faces.

In the end, the teenagers relented and organized a worship time that was quite traditional—and, I might add, acceptable. The adults praised them.

Every now and again, however, I have to laugh at the way children and teenagers reveal the limitations and oddities of our adult ways of thinking about faith. Once, when I was talking to a group of children, I asked the question, "What is faith?"

A little girl raised her hand. "Faith is believing in something that you know ain't true," she said.

There may be more adults who adhere to that line of reasoning than we might imagine. At least, I have my suspicions that this is the case. Many people seem to think that faith is about believing in doctrines and creeds that we can barely swallow, about keeping rules and regulations or adhering to certain brands of theology. Many folks regard faith as a kind of God-sanctioned lottery, a means of keeping some people out while others claim the grand prize. Still others may think of faith as a kind of panacea or medicine that is supposed to make us feel better about things.

Faith, however, is not a commodity or a feeling. Faith is not a crapshoot or a panacea for the ills of life. Faith, rather, draws us out of our self-centeredness and allows us to focus upon the needs of others. Faith looks to a power and a love higher than humanity. Most of all, I believe that faith makes a difference in the everyday affairs of living.

I was reminded of this reality in my own life a few years back (and the reality of how difficult it is to actually live the faith I profess). I had concluded worship on a Sunday morning, had gathered my coat and scarf, and was about to leave the building when an unfamiliar voice greeted me from behind: "Are you the pastor?"

Now, understand, a pastor learns to recognize voices very quickly in the parish, and this voice had an unusual accent and lilt. I turned to meet the stranger I knew was behind me—a stocky fellow with a big smile, gray corduroy pants and a thin jacket with holes in it.

"Pardon me?" I asked, realizing I was likely to hear a long story of sadness and gloom.

"Someone told me you were the pastor," the fellow said, extending a hand.

We greeted one another and I asked quickly what he needed, since I was not in the mood to talk. A closer inspection, however, revealed that he needed much. His shoes were ripped at the soles and one of his pant legs was torn in a jagged **Z**.

"I was wondering if you could help me with a little food money," he said. "I was on my way to South Carolina, heading down there to attend my grandmother's funeral, when my car broke down about a mile up the street. I used up all my money trying to get the car towed and repaired, but I've had to leave it for junk. I'm trying to get up a little money for a bus ticket. But right now I'm lookin' for a bite to eat."

His story sounded familiar. I had heard it before—different people, but the same story.

Grandmother dead or dying. Car breaks down. No money. SOS. Need money for bus ticket and/or food. Preferably both.

At the monthly clergy gatherings we had often talked about this scenario: What do you do when someone uses the old grandmother-dying ploy? Answer: If you know what to do then you know too much.

For some reason, however, as I listened to this man and looked into his eyes (never look into someone's eyes unless you intend to help), I believed his story. And more than that, I believed in him.

"What's your name?" I asked, breaking another rule (never ask a stranger his name unless you really want to know him).

"Willie," he told me.

"Willie," I said. "I'm going to take you out to lunch."

Together we stepped into the bitter cold. Willie immediately crossed his arms over his chest as we walked toward the car. We gathered ourselves inside, and I began to drive toward the nearest fast-food establishment.

As we neared the parking lot, however, I could not bring myself to turn in. Taking Willie to a fast-food restaurant just didn't seem hospitable; it didn't seem right. I took a turn and drove toward home. "Why don't you eat with me and the family?" I asked aloud, almost hoping that he would decline and save me the trouble of explaining things to my wife.

Willie hesitated but agreed.

The closer we got to the house, the more I became aware of Willie as a person. I broke another rule (don't talk to a stranger unless you want to know him as a friend). I asked about his family, his home, whether he had any goals in life. He told me about a failed marriage, a teenage son whom he loved very much, and his skills as an artist.

"I've always wanted to make a living as a painter or an illustrator," Willie told me. "I don't have any formal training, but I'm good enough to make a living with my art if someone would give me the chance."

Willie talked, and I believed him.

When we arrived at my house, I knocked on the front door and hurriedly explained the situation to my wife.

"Honey, I've brought a stranger home for dinner. Kill the fatted calf. Set an extra place at the table. Put rings on his fingers and bells on his toes. Make him feel welcome and show him how charming you are."

Actually, I had to explain the situation to my wife within the soundproof confines of the bathroom. She just didn't know Willie the way I did. But all turned out well.

Together we sat down to eat an exquisite Sunday-afternoon feast comprised of cold-cut sandwiches and canned soup. No one was complaining, however. Especially not Willie.

Things really got interesting, however, when my five-year-old daughter sprang from her shyness and began asking questions: "Who is this turkey?" "What's he doing sitting in my chair?" "Why is he drinking from our cups and eating with our spoons?" "Is this guy going to spend the night, or what?" "Uh, Daddy, did you know this guy has a rip in his pants?"

As soon as my daughter mentioned the pants, and while I was apologizing to Willie, my wife went into the bedroom and emerged a few minutes later, carrying an assortment of clothing—my clothing! "Here, try these on," she told Willie. "I think they'll fit you. You can change in the bathroom."

I realized right away that my wife had broken another rule: Never give clothing—especially underwear—to a stranger unless you intend to bond with him.

Willie left the table looking like a tattered waif, and made his grand entrance a few minutes later looking like the prince of Bulgaria. He was dressed in my finest attire: a pair of pants from J. C. Penney, a shirt from Kmart, socks and shoes from Sam's Club. *By golly,* I thought, *he looks pretty damn good in those duds.* And to think that my wife and child had to make the switch for me.

A few minutes later, I arranged to take Willie to the bus depot. Another pastor had agreed to pick up the bus fare, and I gave Willie a small wad of bills to tide him over for a week or so.

We were about to leave the house when Willie said, "Wait a minute. I can't leave until I give *you* something."

Give me something? What did he have in mind?

Willie went over to the desk near the telephone and pulled out a ballpoint pen and a piece of paper. He sat down at the kitchen table, sighed, and then began to draw. All of us watched—especially my daughter, who, from the time she learned to talk, had told us daily that she wanted to be an artist when she grew up.

Willie moved the ink in long lines down the paper, made circles and triangles and ellipses. He cross-hatched and dabbed at the paper like it was an expensive canvas. Sometimes he smeared the ink with the tip of his finger or moved the wetness around with a wad of tissue paper.

At first the drawing was just an inanimate thing, a mere lump. But gradually it took shape. Forms grew. The paper began to breathe. Eyes and hands and feet appeared, and then the totality of the vision that Willie had plucked from his mind to bring to life on the paper began to emerge.

At last he handed the ink drawing to my daughter and, in a final flourish, signed his name at the bottom. My wife and I were astonished at his talent and the small thing he had created: a picture of a field mouse dangling from a bent sunflower stalk. The mouse, his eyes and ears wide with surprise, also portrayed a more subtle strength, for Willie had managed to imbue the little rodent with an inner fortitude, a kind of faith that seemed to say, "Hang on, baby, you're going to make it."

My daughter took the drawing, again breaking another rule: Never accept a gift from a stranger unless you plan to call him a friend.

Willie said his good-byes, and then I drove him to the bus depot, breaking a final rule: Never say good-bye to a stranger at a bus depot unless you plan to remain friends for life. But as soon as I arrived back home, my daughter was asking her usual round of questions. "Who was that man?" "Why was he here?" "Why did we give him food and clothes?" "Why did you take him in your car?" "Why?"

At first I tried to answer her questions in my usual, grown-up manner.

"It was practical," I explained. "He needed some food, and I was coming home to eat anyway. He needed clothes, and I had a few extra things in my closet that I wasn't wearing. It was no big deal."

"But why did you bring him *here?*" she wanted to know.

I tried to explain how things were. "I was leaving the church when he showed up. I'm the pastor and I thought he needed some help. So I brought him here."

"But why did *we* have to help him?" she pressed.

Finally, unable to get around the issue, I remembered that my daughter and the other children had sung "Jesus Loves Me" at church that morning. That song made sense. It was the answer I was looking for.

"Well," I explained, "I guess we helped Willie because that is what our faith tells us to do. Jesus loves us. You know, like the song says. Jesus loves Willie, too. So why shouldn't we? It's just as simple as that."

Faith works best when it's childlike. When it becomes too complex or fancy the answers don't seem to work—especially not with strangers.

Faith is a way of living. It is the way in which we approach God and our neighbors. Faith opens the door and lets the stranger in, trusting that God would do the very same thing.

Now, if you really want a lesson in faith, watch a circus.

Last summer my wife and I took the kids to the "big top" to witness a three-ring show featuring elephants, lions and an impressive array of specialty acts. We saw women swinging from the high trapeze. One fellow was shot out of a cannon into a net on the other side of the auditorium. We saw women dangling by clenched teeth at the end of a rope.

The most impressive act, however, was on the high wire. Here we witnessed the greatest act of faith in the entire circus—if you want to define faith as absolute trust. Walking gingerly on a taut wire, a husband and wife made their way across the thin abyss from opposite ends, crossing over one another in the middle. Then, in a great act of trust, the husband hoisted his wife onto his shoulders and walked the full length of the wire.

There was no safety net.

Faith has often been described as a leap, as trust involving an element of risk. It's as if we put all of our cards on the table at once while knowing full well we will not be dealt another hand.

That's why faith is the stuff of the strong and the brave. Having faith involves fortitude and determination. Having faith in someone or something is an act of courage, not weakness.

I've known many people who have relied upon their faith during times of great sorrow and pain. Their faith enabled them to face their situation with courage and confidence. I'm not certain they would have made it through the tough times without their faith.

My friend Emma would know something about this kind of faith. She and her four children were abandoned by her husband, forced into bankruptcy, and moved to a home that was far too small for their needs. Emma kept the family together on a small salary, and there were days when food was sparse at the table and other needs went unmet. But Emma persevered with her faith, always believing that God would see her through to another day, that God would keep the family together and provide for their needs.

No, her life didn't turn around on a dime, and there were more tears and bitterness along the way. But circumstances did change. Faith persevered. Life did improve with time.

I also think of the year a prominent family in the congregation lost their father in a freak accident. It was near Christmas, and their father's presents were already wrapped and neatly stacked beneath the tree. That was a difficult Christmas for that family, and I imagine there were silence and tears when the blessed morning finally arrived and their father was not there to celebrate with them.

But I will not forget the act of faith on the part of the two sons. They told me that on New Year's Eve they had taken their father's gifts to a local men's shelter and given them away, gift by gift.

"It's what Dad taught us to do," they said. "That's what he believed: Give when you don't feel like giving. He would have done the same thing."

Call it a spirit of charity if you like, but, for the sons, distributing their father's gifts was every bit as much an act of faith as an act of giving. Their faith told them it was possible for the spirit of their father to live on through their giving. And they gave.

I think, when we get down to the essence of what faith is all about and why so many people have a faith and a tradition that is meaningful to them, it has something to do with a desire to be good, to know good, even when life isn't good to us. Faith is taking all the storms of life and transforming them into showers of blessings. Faith is about transforming our nasty circumstances into hopeful beginnings and new opportunities. Or, as the old saying goes, faith teaches us that when life gives us lemons, we can make lemonade.

No amount of wishful thinking can give a person faith. Faith, rather, is something that wells up from some deep recess within. Faith is also the foundation of life. Where would any of us be without the essence of faith in daily life? Marriage is built on faith. So are many business relationships. Parents trust children, and children trust parents—this is faith. A fellow climbs onto the back of an unbridled horse— this is faith (maybe more so on the part of the horse). A woman who falls in love with a man has faith (though maybe also a bit of bad judgment). When diplomats get together and shake hands over a peace accord—this is faith.

If you and I can learn to trust each other in all these ways and more, why should it feel strange to have faith in the creator of the universe?

Now for something about my own faith. Folks are always asking me what I believe about this or that, as if I am supposed to pass some sort of litmus test or know the answers to the riddles of the universe. Religious leaders of other faiths receive this same treatment. When folks have problems with their cars, they naturally go to mechanics. When they have a problem with their urinary tracts, they make appointments with urologists. When they want to know what to believe or how they should believe or how they should respond to a certain predicament, they riffle through the yellow pages for clergy who are supposed to be experts.

But I say from the outset: I am not an expert. That is what I believe is true of myself.

Yet, folks still like to ask me. So I will tell you a bit about my faith and what I believe is true about life.

First, my faith is always changing and expanding. There are many facets of faith that I believe more strongly now than ever before. I believe in the immutable grace of God, for instance, and in the possibility of reconciliation between people. More specifically, as a Christian, I believe in one man—Jesus of Nazareth. He is my example, if you want to count self-sacrifice and humility and gentleness as desirable human traits. Jesus also condemned religious professionals (like me!) and religious establishments (like the church!), and this comforts me more than I can say. God knows I need less of myself and far less of the institution of the church if I'm ever to find more of God and learn how to love my neighbor.

I also believe in listening to children and playing in sand-boxes. I believe in letting the little things slide and giving an all-out effort when something really matters to others. And I believe in laughing a lot, and writing people thank-you notes, and doing yard work as little as possible.

I'm also big on listening to others—especially when I don't agree with them. And I'm certain that I can learn much from other faith traditions. And I really believe that we all should love and care for each other a whole lot more than we do, especially our enemies and those who live on the fringes of society.

Most of all, this is a faith that I try to live each day. If I can't live it, I can't really say that I believe it.

Not long ago, I was given the opportunity to articulate many of these beliefs when I spoke at an outdoor gathering in a city park golf course. Folks were lining up to walk or run for some worthy cause, and the powers that be had asked me to say a few words before the beginning of the event as a kind of inspirational device.

It was a rainy morning, but surprisingly, a large number of people had rallied for the cause under umbrellas and trench coats. Someone handed me a megaphone. When I talked into the blasted thing, it squealed.

In four short minutes I told stories about the need for help-ing our neighbors and coming to the aid of a friend and band-ing together for greater causes than our own selfish needs. I also told stories of faith and made reference, on one or two

occasions, to our human need for love and our need for God—
only I didn't say it quite like that, I'm sure. I don't remember
a single sentence of the presentation, only the stories.

When it was over and the walkers departed and I was left
standing alone in the rain, a young man approached, looking
as lonely and forlorn as myself. Without an umbrella or plastic hood, the young man's hair and face were sopped and
dripping. But he didn't bat an eye.

"Hey, let me ask you something," he said from a small distance. "You really believe all that stuff you were talking about
back there? All those stories?"

I had no idea where the conversation might be going. I
answered from the heart. "Yeah. Most of the time. And if I
don't believe it, I'd like to."

He smiled in the rain. "Me, too."

We were walking toward the clubhouse under a dismal sky.
In the far distance, it thundered; gray mist permeated the air.

As we approached the shelter and smelled hot chocolate
rising from Styrofoam cups, he turned and offered me an act
of faith.

"Hey, you got any more stories?"

When I think of faith, I hear the words of simple songs like
"Jesus Loves Me"; I think of finger painting and brightly
colored balloons and streamers. And I think of stories—the
kind of stories Jesus told—tales about people who learned
how to forgive a debt, or how to help a neighbor, or how to
keep on knocking even when the doors are closed and the
lights have been turned out for the night.

Faith has to do with becoming a part of those stories, with seeing ourselves as a part of the drama, of God's work in this world. Faith is learning how to live the words we sing and the poems we write and the creeds we profess.

When your life and mine come to a close, and the words have all been spoken, and our bodies delivered to our final resting places, this is when our faith will wither, or sprout roots and grow. Your life and mine will tell a story, and we will be part of a much longer and larger story that begins and ends with the One who made us. And the people we leave behind will remember us for the way we lived for others, and the qualities that distinguished us, and the faith we possessed. They will be drawn, not to our own goodness, but to the One who is good.

This is the true faith. This is the life. This is the old, old story.

5

Hope

Hope is grief's best music

—traditional proverb

A few days before Christmas, the phone rang at four o'clock on a Sunday morning. I answered groggily and listened as a maternity nurse at the local hospital apologized for calling at such an ungodly hour.

"Reverend," she began, "I'm sorry, but we've got an unusual situation down here in labor and delivery. There's an expectant mother who wants to get married. She's nearly hysterical! She has a valid marriage license, her boyfriend is here, and they want to get married before the baby arrives!"

Shaking the sleep from my eyes, I nearly dropped off again, thinking the call was a prank.

"Let me see if I heard you correctly," I said. "You've got a woman down there who's about to give birth?"

"Could be any minute."

"She has a valid marriage license?"

"That's right."

"The groom is there?"

"Standing by."

"And they want to get married at a time like this?"

"Well, you see," the nurse explained, "they want the baby to have the same last name as the father. The mother isn't cooperating with the delivery process. She's hysterical and quite adamant about getting married before the baby arrives."

I could scarcely believe what I was hearing. Talk about last-minute wedding plans. "Why are you calling *me?*" I asked, longing for a return to my warm, cozy bed and a few more hours of sleep. Why hadn't the nurse picked on the Presbyterian pastor for a change?

"Well," the nurse answered apologetically, "we've called every pastor in town. No one will perform the ceremony. And you're the last sucker we could find in the phone book. *Please* help us!"

Glancing at the clock, I realized that I would have to rise in three hours anyway. I had never officiated at a birthing-room wedding before and . . . *What the hell*, I thought, *how can I pass this up?*

"I'll be there as soon as I get dressed," I told the maternity nurse.

"Make it quick!" she shot back. "This baby isn't going to wait long."

Jumping into the shower, I began to soap my armpits, shave my face and shampoo my hair—all at the same time. I finished in thirty seconds: a new shower record. But when I looked in the mirror I discovered that I had shaved one armpit, shampooed my face and soaped my scalp to a stiff froth. My face was nicked and bleeding in several places. I threw on a suit and tie while sticking dots of toilet paper to my razor-damaged cheeks, grabbed my handy-dandy book of marriage ritual, and tossed my aching body into the front seat of the car.

Racing across town, I shot through stop signs, ran red lights and skidded to a halt outside the emergency room entrance at the hospital. Bounding into the maternity wing, I was met at the doors by the same nurse who had talked with me on the telephone only minutes before. "We'd better run," she prodded. "The baby is starting to crown!"

Jogging down the corridor, the nurse led me around the corner to a birthing room (the same room, in fact, where my wife would give birth to our first child a year later). Removing clumps of toilet paper from my chin, I crashed through the door, the aura of matrimonial bliss greeting me in all its splendor.

The bride, draped in a pure white sheet, was reclining at a forty-five degree angle in bed, her swollen feet in the stirrups, great beads of sweat rolling down her cheeks. The groom, smiling broadly by the side of her bed, seemed genuinely proud of the results of his manhood. Two nurses—on either side of the blessed couple—served as witnesses along with the father figure: a mustached doc holding a ragged pair of sterile forceps.

Realizing the sacredness of the moment, the doctor momentarily forfeited his instrument of torture and, as he stepped around me, whispered in my ear, "Whatever you're gonna say, Reverend, make it quick!"

What happened next is something of a blur in my mind. But to the best of my recollection, the wedding ceremony transpired within a two-minute time frame, accompanied, every twenty seconds, by the anguished strains of the bride as she withheld her urge to push through the gut-wrenching contractions.

"Will you have this woman to be your wife?" I asked the nameless groom.

"I will," he answered joyfully, staring down into the angry eyes of his bride-to-be.

"Will you have this man to be your husband?" I asked the writhing bride.

"Ugggghhhh-hhuuugghhh," she answered. (I took this as an affirmation.)

"Then I now announce that you are husband and wife together . . . etc., and so forth. You may now kiss the bride."

The groom leaned down to kiss his bride but recoiled as her fist came up to meet his nose.

Now that the ceremony was over, and since I had never been witness to a live birth before, I decided to skip the reception and retreated into the hallway, shaken but unbowed. The new husband followed me.

"How much do I owe you, pastor?" he asked, reaching for his wallet.

I was about to say something facetious like, "Mister, there is no amount of money you could pay me for what I just witnessed in there!"—but I stopped short. In that moment I recognized something in his eyes, a tear perhaps, or a glint of melancholy, that revealed the depth of his poverty and his embarrassment. I realized that I had just wed two people, impoverished in many ways, who were now bringing a new life into an uncertain world. The situation seemed so bizarre that it bordered on the laughable.

The man now extended an open wallet, offering me a few dollars to ease his pain. "How much do I owe you?" he asked again.

I took a deep breath. "Save your money for the baby," I told him, trying to smile.

Slowly, he folded his wallet and slipped it into his hip pocket. He extended his hand and said, "thank you."

We shook hands and I watched him disappear into the birthing room along with the eager doctor. I waited in the foyer for a few minutes, watching the nurses scurry back and forth with the necessary articles that accompany the pains of birth. Then there was silence around me.

Backing out of the maternity wing, I regained my composure and strode down a narrow glass corridor toward my car. Outside it had started to snow: large delicate flakes suspended in lamplight, brilliant as jewels.

As the automatic doors opened and I stepped into the cold, I paused in the darkness to gaze upon a simple crèche erected near the emergency room entrance. There was mother Mary. The infant Jesus. Wise men and shepherds. A sprinkling of sheep. An angel.

But it was Joseph I noticed most of all.

Here was a poor man who harbored the same expressions, the same doubts and fears and poverties, as the father and groom I had left behind. I waited in the darkness and gazed into the eyes of the ceramic figure, noted the utter humanness of the features, and became aware, at last, of my own being. From a loudspeaker overhead, I heard the faint words of a hymn I had sung countless times since my childhood. But somehow the words seemed new, fresh—as if I were hearing them for the first time:

> O little town of Bethlehem,
> How still we see thee lie;
> Above thy deep and dreamless sleep
> the silent stars go by.
> Yet in thy dark streets shineth
> the everlasting light;
> the hopes and fears of all the years
> are met in thee tonight.

There, standing on frozen ground outside the emergency room entrance, I pondered the extreme realities of hope and fear.

Birth. Life. Death. The spectrum of existence. And it occurred to me then that every person who has ever lived has needed the space and longing called hope. Hope compels us to welcome a new life into the world, though we know full well the perils and dangers and risks of bringing any life into the world. Hope drives us into the future when all seems bleak and despairing. And hope is, in essence, the deep-down, in-the-guts struggle of human existence that compels one person to love another, to take a chance on happiness, to reach out a hand in friendship.

Every person longs for hope. And yet, it is as elusive as a rainbow.

In my experience, hope is the one thing so many of us lack. We have faith, an ample supply of love. We have the necessary skills and abilities. We have desire. But hope—the vision to see beyond what *is* to what *might be*—often eludes the human spirit.

In fact, I have heard many people say, in the face of un-settling odds, "It's hopeless." But hope, by virtue of its very definition, is a speculative venture. Hope plays against the odds; it attaches itself to something greater and higher than human achievement and knowledge. Hope looks for the possibilities in the impossible.

But it doesn't come easy.

I know one of my first adventures in hope didn't fare so well. I was four years old at the time, and my parents had told me that we were going to move to another town—which meant, for me, another world, another universe. But all I could think about was my friend Alan, who lived across the street. Would I ever see him again? Would we still be friends?

These questions haunted me. I had no way of knowing what moving to another town would mean. So I allowed the spirit of hope to creep into my life; I nourished it daily with prayer to an unseen God, waiting for any sign of reprieve.

Perhaps my parents would not move after all. Parents sometimes changed their minds, didn't they? Maybe the moving van would not arrive. I clung to a thousand hopes.

But, of course, I learned that hope is more than just day-dreams and wishes. Hope is not a magic star, a prayer or a por-tent. Hope has its own rewards. By hoping, I was freeing myself to find the strength to change and grow. I learned that hope has everything to do with the future and very little to do with the past.

But sometimes we receive it backward.

Not long ago, I sat down with my children on a rainy Saturday afternoon to watch *Willy Wonka and the Chocolate*

Factory—a wonderful movie about a young boy named Charlie who dreams of finding one of five golden tickets inside a Wonka chocolate bar, a ticket that will allow him to visit the infamous and reclusive Willy Wonka himself. The only problem is, Charlie is poor. Wonka has produced millions of candy bars, and all but one of the golden tickets has been found.

Charlie's hope, however, is not an empty imagining of what might be. Charlie not only dreams of finding the golden ticket, he strives to make it a reality—namely by buying and eating as many Wonka bars as possible. He works hard to earn extra money to buy candy. He scours the town gutters for coins. He does not allow his perseverance to waver in the face of overwhelming odds.

Charlie, of course, finds the remaining golden ticket; he wins because he gives hope a chance to succeed. His unwavering efforts are like wings.

In the end, not only does Charlie get to see Willy Wonka and tour his fabulous chocolate factory, he becomes the heir apparent of the entire operation. And why? Because his heart is pure.

Call *Willy Wonka and the Chocolate Factory* a children's movie if you like, but it is every bit as much a morality play as anything else. It is a movie about true hope—the kind of hope we adults often forfeit when our dreams don't come true, but which, if we only had the gumption to strive against great odds, would produce spectacular results. Hope is often made manifest in effort.

Life is difficult enough. Without hope, it is nearly impossible. In fact, human achievement and advancement are nearly always connected to hope.

Take Thomas Edison, for instance. Here was a man who invented many of the modern conveniences we take for granted. But he wasn't just a great inventor or a committed scientist. He had vision. He saw things around him that other people could not see. He envisioned new uses for common objects. Indeed, he was as much a visionary as he was a pioneer, an inventor who made the future a present reality.

People who have hope often have great vision. They are risk takers. They are not afraid of failure. They know that hope has many faces and facets to it: Things may not turn out the way they envision them, but they are willing to trust the serendipitous nature of life.

This is true not only for scientists and inventors and dreamers, but for anyone who has a problem that needs the nourishment of hope. Sometimes, hope is all we can carry with us and all that gets us through the tough times. Hope is another day, or another hour, or another try.

Somewhere out there, a woman named Daisy is a living example of this reality. I met Daisy when I was a young hospital chaplain. She was a patient on my floor who had been paralyzed from the waist down in an automobile accident.

The first time I entered Daisy's room, I sensed an aura of despair and depression—the lights were turned low, there were no sounds, no cards or letters or flowers. There seemed to be no evidence of visitors. Daisy lay in bed with her back to the door. I walked to the opposite side of the room so I could see her face and introduced myself.

Silence.

I made comments about the hospital, asked about the kind of care she had been receiving. There was no reply; her face was expressionless. I waited a while in the darkness—just stood there and didn't say a word. After several minutes, I told her that I would come back to see her the next day.

The following evening my visit was much the same, but with one notable exception. At the end of my brief visit, when I told Daisy that I would return to visit her again, she emitted a slight sound, a kind of affirming groan.

Day after day, as I visited Daisy, I saw small, visible changes in her outlook and demeanor. She began to talk. She kept the lights on in her room. A few cards and letters appeared. She learned how to pull herself up whenever a visitor entered the room, and she began to initiate conversations. She asked me to pray with her. She told me about her therapy, what she had achieved that morning, how she was looking forward to being released from the hospital.

Eventually, that day did arrive. One evening I walked into Daisy's room and found a vacant bed with a note attached to the headboard: "Thanks for everything. Please write me."

Later I asked the doctor, "What made the difference for Daisy?"

"Daisy needed an operation to get well," he told me. "Even though she had no chance of ever walking again, she had to let go of her anger and despair and find a reason to live. Gradually, she found the hope in a hopeless situation and decided that she could overcome and go on with her life."

"You sound like a theologian," I said.

"That's your line of work," he said with a laugh. "But I've learned a few things about the human spirit over the years. I never operate on a person unless the patient believes she will survive the operation. Hope and confidence are very important ingredients in the recovery process. If a patient thinks she's going to die, she just might die. People who want to live, who have hope to go on living, these people are going to recover. They may not return to the level of life they previously knew and enjoyed, but they are going to recover. I've seen it many times."

More and more, we read about the connection between hope and healing. When a person lives for tomorrow, he or she has found the will to live. Healing may have as much to do with the emotional and psychological state of an individual as it does the physical.

In the PBS series with Bill Moyers, *Healing and the Mind*, one doctor made the statement that fear negatively affects our physical well-being. He pointed out that, although there is no medical evidence to support such a hypothesis, most doctors believe that the mental and emotional state of an individual does affect the healing processes of the body. As a clergyman, I, too, have seen evidence of this. I have witnessed how hope nurtures people through the tough times—not only physical illnesses, but tragedies, divorces, job losses, addictions, family stresses, and a host of emotional and spiritual scars.

Over the years, I've met some very hopeful people who have emerged from enormous tragedies and losses with an unbelievable spirit and zest for life. There seems to be no way to explain this strength other than the resiliency of hope. And often, ironically enough, it seems the people who have had the most heartaches in life are the most hopeful of all.

Recently, at a men's gathering, I met a fellow who had grown up in a government housing project. As I heard him tell his story, the hope that sustained him through all those difficult years impressed me. Even as a child, he knew that someday he would leave the projects and make a life for himself. He had grown up never doubting this vision and hope for a single moment.

Another woman I know has survived tremendous personal losses: the sudden death of a child, the death of her parents, a bitter divorce. All within the span of a year. And yet she is one of the most hopeful and positive people I know.

When you and I experience life's difficulties and challenges, we have two options: We can embrace cynicism and defeat, or we can cling to hope and a positive vision of tomorrow. Hope truly makes a world of difference because, even if our circumstances remain the same, *we* can be changed. We can find the strength to overcome with the help of family and friends, and we can grow to become whole individuals.

Sometimes hope has divine qualities.

There is a story about Pope John Paul II, probably apocryphal, detailing his first venture into the city of Rome. One day he told his entourage, "I'm going for a walk." He put on his red shoes and his robe, took his staff in hand, and set out across Saint Peter's square. Soon he came to the walls of Vatican City. As he pushed on through the gates, one of his bodyguards told him, "Holy Father, you must be careful. Beyond these walls it will be difficult for us to protect you. There are all manner of evils in Rome."

But the pope answered, "God has called me to go to the people."

As soon as the pope and his entourage exited Vatican City, they came upon the poor and the outcast of Rome. The Holy Father went from person to person, blessing as he walked.

Farther on, they came across a man who was blind. The Holy Father blessed him.

At last, as they entered the heart of Rome, people recognized the pope and came swarming for his blessing. Children, mothers, fathers, the elderly—all came and knelt before the pope. Many sought to touch the garments of the Holy Father.

As the pope walked on he came to a prison. "I must go in there," the pope told his entourage. They begged him to reconsider. But the Holy Father pressed on. Once inside the prison, guards and inmates crowded near the cell doors, reaching out their hands for the blessing of God. Going from cell to cell, the pope blessed the inmates and at last came to a huge iron door that looked as if it had not been opened for centuries. "I must go in there," he told the prison guards.

"Oh, no, Holy Father," the prison guards begged. "You do not want to go behind that door. That is where we keep the most dangerous and violent criminals of Rome: murderers, rapists, child molesters. Please, you do not want to go in there. It is too dangerous."

But the pope insisted. "Open the door," he told the guards.

The huge iron door opened slowly, squeaking on its rusted hinges. Surrounded by bodyguards, the pope stepped into the utter darkness, straining to see the huddled figures of men who lay on the floor in filth and decay. A switch was thrown, and a beam of light illuminated the Holy Father.

Suddenly, from out of the darkness, a man screamed and came running toward the pope. But before he could touch the Holy Father, one of the bodyguards stepped forward and drove the man to the ground with a mighty blow to the head. Struggling to his knees, the inmate reached for the robes of the pope with trembling hands, blood streaking his forehead. At last he embraced the pope and began to sob, "Oh, Holy Father, tell me, tell me: Is there any hope for me?" Calmly the Holy Father reached down, touched the man and said, "My son, there is hope for us all."

Hope is the light that enters the darkness—even the darkness and despair of a prison cell. Hope embraces us with God's love when all seems lost. Hope touches us where we hurt—in our sorrows and losses and failures.

Hope, if it grants us anything, gives us the ability to believe that change is possible. Even the insurmountable can . . . might . . . be overcome. Miracles can happen, situations might change. We might be changed.

Let me tell you about a man named Peter Niewick. Several years ago he sat in a doctor's office, waiting for the results of some lab work. The doctor entered, sat down next to Peter Niewick and his wife, tapped his clipboard and said, "Mr. Niewick, I'm afraid I have some bad news. You have cancer. And your prognosis is not good. I think we should begin treatment as soon as possible."

Stunned to silence, Peter Niewick and his wife could scarcely believe what they had heard. To make matters worse, they had just finalized some extensive vacation plans with good friends, a trip to the northwest states, which they had been looking forward to for years. They talked about these plans with the doctor, who agreed that the trip might be very beneficial to them both. Peter Niewick would begin his cancer treatments when he returned from the vacation.

A week later, Peter Niewick found himself standing on the deck of an enormous lodge, looking out across a wide expanse of beautiful forest. Far down in the valley, a crystalline lake glistened in the sun. Above, a majestic mountain rose toward a sky of deepest blue. Peter Niewick's wife, taken with the splendor of the place, went inside the lodge to make a reservation for the following year.

Moved by his wife's act of hope, Peter Niewick wept as he gazed upon the powerful majesty of the place. A friend moved near. "What's wrong, Pete?" he wanted to know.

Taking a deep breath, Peter Niewick tried to explain. "Look around," he said. "Look at that mountain, that lake, all these trees, this huge lodge. It's just unreal. Everything here is going to last forever. My wife's inside making reservations for next year and I don't even know if I'm going to be alive. Everything here is permanent and I'm so fragile."

Peter Niewick and his wife completed that vacation with their friends and returned home. The cancer treatments began. And, at last, even those came to an end.

One day, nearly a year later, Peter Niewick and his wife sat in the same doctor's office awaiting the results of the most recent lab tests. The doctor entered the office, sat down, tapped his clipboard a couple of times and then said, "Mr. Niewick, I have great news for you. You've beaten the odds. We can find no trace of cancer in your body. Have a good life."

The news came as Peter Niewick and his wife were planning their annual vacation. But the Niewicks never did return to that beautiful lodge in the mountains.

Why?

Because it wasn't there. You see, the lodge where the Niewicks had planned to stay was called Harmony Falls Lodge. That beautiful lake in the valley was called Spirit

Lake and the mountain was Mount Saint Helens. When it erupted, everything for miles and miles around was completely obliterated: the lodge, the lake, the sprawling forests and most of the mountain itself.

Those things that Peter Niewick had believed were permanent and unmoving were now nothing but rubble. Yet his life, which he had believed to be weak and fleeting, now remained.

Hope has that potential. It stretches our boundaries, takes our life from us and then gives it back again.

6

Love

Live thou thy life beneath the making sun
Till Beauty, Truth and Love in thee are one.

—Robert Bridges

In 1969, Leo Buscaglia was teaching education courses at the University of Southern California when he received word that one of his students, a bright and dedicated young woman, had committed suicide. She was only twenty years old, had grown up in a middle-class family, and was popular, beautiful and intelligent. Her future seemed as promising as any student's on campus. Her entire life was before her.

In an effort to understand why this young woman had taken her own life, Leo Buscaglia leafed through a pile of term papers he had recently graded. In the pile, he found the paper that belonged to this young woman—a paper she had never received. Buscaglia read with great interest the notes he had made in the margins of her essay: "A very fine paper. Perceptive, intelligent and sensitive. It indicates your ability to apply what you have learned to your 'real' life."

Real life? What did he actually know about her real life? Obviously he knew nothing at all about her feelings, her struggles, her doubts and insecurities. He knew nothing about the deep sadness and sense of futility that had crept into her heart.

This young woman's death caused Leo Buscaglia to ponder why so many people, even young people who have their entire future ahead of them, seem to be searching for love and meaning in life. Why was it that students could talk freely about sex and responsibility, about death and hope and careers . . . and yet miss the essence of what life is all about? These questions perplexed him and compelled him to take action.

That next semester he decided to offer a class that he called "Love Class." Right away he received remarks from his colleagues. Some professors dismissed his class as pure fluff. Others laughed. "No one will take your class," they said. "And besides, what's academic about the subject of love? And how in the world are you going to teach it?"

The university refused to pay Buscaglia for teaching this class, so he decided to offer it on his own time, free of the restraints of salary. That semester, more than one hundred students enrolled in the class. In time, it became one of the most popular classes offered on the campus of USC.

Growing out of his years teaching this class, Leo Buscaglia wrote a classic volume entitled, simply, *Love*. In this work he makes hundreds of observations about this thing we call love—why we crave love, why we want to love someone else, why we find it difficult to speak of love, and why love is, above all else, sometimes mysterious and elusive.

I think Leo Buscaglia is correct. Love is elusive. For in spite of our profusion of talk about love, our many songs about love and our movies about love, most people are not entirely certain what love is. And most of us find it equally difficult to express our feelings of love in any kind of coherent manner. I suppose that is one of the reasons why greeting card companies are so prolific—we just don't know how to say "I love you," so we search for words on a greeting card to summarize our feelings.

Why do we find it difficult to talk about love, to express it, to write about it?

I think it has to do with the fact that love is not a subject that can be readily discussed in any type of intellectual manner. We don't normally talk about love like we talk about other subjects. I think this is because love is not a noun. Love is a verb. When you and I try to talk about love as a commodity, we can't quite grasp it. But when we experience love, when we receive it . . . well, we know it.

Gandhi once said, "There is no love where there is no will." Love is not just a feeling or an attitude. Love is an action. Love reaches out, steps out, speaks out, cries out and sometimes holds out. Love perseveres because that is our desire. Like a waterfall, love is always moving—it is not stagnant like a pond. Ironically, the more love we try to hoard for ourselves, the less love we receive. The more love we give away, the more we find.

Over the years, I've collected newspaper and magazine accounts of people who have lived sacrificially or who have performed great acts of love. And what amazes me about the human spirit is, surprisingly, not the scarcity of such acts, but their abundance. It seems that every week I read a story about someone who is moved by the power of love, who is compelled to take a stand, make a choice or take a risk for the sake of another.

Take, for instance, a recent story about a little boy and his sister who live in Illinois. It seems that the older sister had a rare form of leukemia and would need, among other things, several blood transfusions to speed her healing. However, she had a rare blood type, and the doctors searched frantically for a matching donor. When it seemed that no donors were going to step forward, the doctors discovered that the girl's younger brother shared the same rare blood type.

The doctor clarified the situation to the family and then approached the six-year-old boy. "Normally we don't take blood from little boys," the doctor explained. "But if you give your blood, you will save your sister's life."

Initially the little boy was hesitant and, naturally, frightened, but after some deep thought he told the doctor, "I want my sister to live."

The next day the doctor prepared to draw the blood. The little boy was placed on a table, the instruments were readied and then the doctor held the needle so the little boy could see it. "Remember," the doctor said, "this may hurt a little bit, but it will save your sister's life."

The little boy swallowed hard and then, meekly, asked a very serious question: "When I give my blood, will I begin to die right away? Will I feel anything when I die?"

Suddenly the doctor and the parents realized that the little boy had not understood the request for blood. He had believed all along that he was exchanging his life for his sister's. And yet he was willing to do it.

Jesus once said, "There is no greater love than this: that one lay down one's life for a friend."

This degree of love, for most of us, can only be understood when we consider a parent's love for a child. Which of us would not sacrifice our own life for that of our children? Who among us would not give a kidney, or an arm or leg for that matter, to spare our children physical pain and anguish?

A couple of years ago, a made-for-television movie depicted a true story about a little boy whose body was wracked by horrible seizures. Week after week, month after month, he suffered as his mother stood by and watched, helplessly. The boy was shuffled from doctor to doctor, from specialist to specialist, from hospital to hospital. But all to no avail.

At last, this little boy was committed to a specialist's care—a doctor who told the mother that he had no alternative but to remove one-half of the boy's brain. Unwilling to accept this procedure for her son, the mother risked everything—even at the threat of serving a prison sentence—and removed her son from the specialist's care. She boarded him on an airplane, flew him across the country, and asked that he be admitted to an experimental program being developed at Johns Hopkins. Love moved her to risk everything for her son, and, in the end, she saved his life. Had she accepted her son's fate without question, had she loved less, her son would no doubt have died.

Love is the only power that can compel us to risk our own lives. And love is the only power that has the potential to heal all the wounds that human beings inflict upon one another.

When you and I consider the power of love, we come to realize that love is most commonly found in the small cracks and spaces of life. Love is the power that compels us to find our future with a person, to forgive, to share the mundane moments of existence.

I believe that most of us, when we think about it, experience love in the little things: helping our spouse with a household chore, squeezing from the same end of the toothpaste tube, sitting on the back porch with our children while eating out of the same bowl of popcorn. That's love.

Love is letting someone else hold the umbrella on a rainy day. Love is forgetting about the argument you had last night and forging ahead with a civil breakfast conversation in the morning. Love is allowing someone else to watch his or her show on the television when there is only one television in the house.

In my estimation, love is composed of many daily decisions, of small matters of the heart and will. Like everything else in life, love is a choice. We choose to fall in love, and we choose to stay in love. Every day is another opportunity to express our love through the little things.

In my estimation, this is where so many relationships begin to go wrong. When we grow to expect only major displays of love, we can miss the little expressions. Love has more to do with all of the minor details of life than it does the major decisions. Sometimes a parent might forget that loving a child means cleaning up a mess now and then, that it means forgiving and sacrificing. A love affair might sour because one person or the other forgets to say thank you. A marriage goes awry because a husband gives more attention to his work than to his wedding anniversary.

Love is in the details. And we know love when we see it.

Sometimes, I suppose, we grow into the habit of believing that love is easy. We fall in love and—*bang!*—we think we don't have to work at love anymore. Quite the opposite is true, however. Love requires even more work than not loving at all. Apathy takes no effort. Love takes everything we've got. Maybe that is why so many people give up on love when the hard work kicks in.

It is difficult to keep on loving a child who throws temper tantrums and makes constant demands on our time and energy. But if not for the power of love, how could anyone survive as a parent? It is difficult to love a spouse who consistently takes more than he or she gives, but then, sacrifice is at the heart of every good marriage. And who would want a marriage without sacrifices?

Yes, love requires far more than any of us have to give. But love is also the most freeing experience of all. When we rest assured of another's love, there is a kind of energy that flows into us, giving us the energy to love all the more. Great loves and great lovers feed off each other. One love reciprocates another.

Love also bears burdens.

Years ago, when I was a college student, I started going to the county jail each week with a group of older men. We went to the jail to talk to those men who were behind bars.

We wanted them to know that they were not forgotten, that others cared about them. We tried to offer words of hope, often from the Bible, and we typically closed by saying a prayer together.

During those many weeks that I frequented that jail, I met men who could have been my neighbors or coworkers. The only difference was, we were on opposite sides of the bars. I met hardened criminals, people who were waiting for their trials to come to court but who could not post bond. I talked with men who were later convicted of murder and rape, of assault and theft, and who were eventually transferred to federal or state prisons to serve lengthy sentences.

Mostly, however, I met men not so unlike myself. During the many weeks that I frequented that jail, I typically met people I knew behind those bars: high school friends, neighbors from my hometown, men I had worked with or conversed with on many occasions. They had made mistakes with the law, found themselves in a scrape and wound up locked in a cell for a few days. Some had problems with drugs or alcohol. Others had tempers. Some vowed to go straight and turn their lives around when they were released. Others didn't care.

Often I wondered where love had entered into their lives. I wondered whether they had ever experienced the unconditional love of a parent or a good friend. One evening I saw my answer.

As I was exiting the building, I noticed a familiar face coming up the steps toward the jail. I recognized the woman right away. She was the mother of a young man who was accused of stealing from a local music store—his first offense. I followed her back into the jail, where, with tears streaming down her cheeks, she apologized to the officers on duty for her son's behavior and explained that she had paid his bail. This money was, no doubt, a significant sum for her, a true sacrifice. But she gave up her own money on the promise that her son would appear at his trial. This mother was heartbroken, burdened by her son's mistake, and I could see this in her eyes.

That's love. There's no way to define it, but we know it when we see it.

Perhaps that is why we are so fascinated by people like Mother Teresa who seem to have put aside all sense of self, who seem able to give themselves away in great doses of compassion. They seem so out of the ordinary, so beyond the pale of ordinary humanity that we feel mystically drawn to emulate their actions. We think, *If only I could love like that, with no regard for self or safety, I would be free of so many worries and cares.*

Why do we feel this tug? What is it that compels us to want to love more deeply, more freely? Why do we aspire to give more of ourselves to others?

I think one answer may be obvious: We were born with the capacity to love. It is our nature. Love is inherited. Hatred, prejudice and greed are taught, but love is natural to our being. Even the most horrible people who have ever lived have loved *someone,* and been loved *by* someone. When we follow a path other than love, we betray the very nature of our humanity— the need that God has placed within every heart.

We are children who want a warm embrace. We crave love. We want to love others. For that is the very nature of God.

I've heard many day-care workers speak of this innate desire and capacity in children. Children naturally want love and acceptance. They long to be held, assured and protected.

Every time I go into my son's day-care room I see this. Children crave words and gestures of appreciation. Sometimes children want to hug. Sometimes they want to snuggle. Always they want to feel the love of an adult around them.

You and I are no different. Deep down we want to love and to be loved. But we often forget this and are turned aside by other cares and concerns that we believe are more important. We forsake our love of others for the love of things, or the love of power, or the love of position.

Why are we so quick to give up on love as adults? Why does love seem so elusive as we grow older?

Perhaps we develop other patterns of behavior, another set of values. Or maybe we consider compassion to be too lofty a goal, more fit for saints and goody-goodies and dreamers than for average folks. Maybe we don't think we're good enough to love so recklessly and completely.

But everyone is capable of loving.

The power of love, if it holds any promise for humanity, is in forgiveness. Without the forgiving touch, the forgiving word, how is love possible? Without forgiveness, what is love worth?

I've heard many older couples speak of love in this vein. They talk about the need to forgive, to not sweat the small stuff in a marriage.

Years back, when I was working with teenagers every week, I organized an event for Valentine's Day. I invited several married couples to serve on a panel. Some of these folks had been married fifty years or more. I thought the teenagers and I might gain much from their wisdom and their insights about love, romance and marriage. We were not disappointed.

In particular, I remember many of their observations about forgiveness and the need to keep love fresh. Here are a few of the most memorable quips:

When you have an argument, even if you know you are right, always say, "I'm sorry."

Never criticize your wife's cooking.

Always be the first to make up when you've had a spat.

Don't forget to put the dog out at night or you'll be sorry in the morning.

Boys, if you must choose between bowling and dancing . . . choose dancing.

Make your husband feel strong, even if he isn't, and he might just live up to it.

Stand up for your spouse when he or she is being criticized by others.

Don't think that problems will go away by themselves— you have to talk them out.

Never forget an anniversary.

Remember that marriage is made up of the little things.

Say "I love you" every day.

I gained much from listening to these older couples. They were genuine and warm, and their memories were inspirational. Everyone seeking to be a better person or parent, a better husband or wife, might do well to find older mentors who have learned the secrets of love.

There is another old adage: In love is no lack.

When we learn to give and receive love well, we find that we have all that we need. There have been many instances in my life when I've witnessed the validity of this insight. I have known families with great wealth who have lacked the simplest of joys and the warmest touches of love. I have known other families who are poor in the material things of life, yet are filled to overflowing with love for one another. Such realities make me wonder who has the greater riches.

In Jewish tradition, there are many stories that provide insight and wisdom about the wonders and riches of love. Among these are the rabbinical tales concerning the creation of the universe. When the rabbis discussed with one another, "Why did God create the world when there is so much evil and deception?" they often reached the same conclusion.

One traditional story goes like this.

After God had finished creating the world and all living things, God decided to make human beings. These beings, however, were to be special, as they would bear the very image of God. The Creator said, "Human beings will have intellect, reason and understanding, just as I do."

Truth approached the Almighty and pleaded, "God, I beg you to reconsider. Why would you create a creature who is capable of telling lies? They will fill your beautiful world with deception and deceit."

Peace, too, came forward and begged the Creator to reconsider the creation of human beings. "God, surely these beings will wreak havoc on the earth. They will war with each other, live by hatred and revenge. They will be guided by their desire for blood, rather than any desire for peace."

While Truth and Peace were talking, Love came along and begged the Almighty to proceed with the creation. "God, because these beings will bear your image, they will have the capacity to do great things. Guided by your Spirit, they will comfort their sick, help the stranger and shelter the orphan. Beings such as these could only bring glory and honor to you, O God."

And so, although God listened to the voices of Truth and Peace, it was because of Love that human beings were created.

Perhaps the rabbis were correct. You and I have the capacity to love in incredible ways. We can go the extra mile, defend the defenseless, risk life and limb for the sake of another. We even have the capacity to give our lives for someone else.

Think about that for a moment.

When someone we love is hurting or dying, there is nothing we wouldn't do to ease their pain or save them from death's grip. As a father, I've thought about this from time to time, and I've come to the conclusion that if my son or daughter were dying, I would give them anything—my heart, my liver, the very breath in my body. I would do the same for my wife. I'd give myself up for anyone I truly loved. So would you.

Of course, we can give our lives in some dramatic fashion to demonstrate our love, or we can take a more common approach: that of giving our lives away gradually, piece by piece, moment by moment. In fact, each of us does that every day. We are all dying for something, or somebody. We are dying for a great many things and for a great many reasons. And some of them have to do with love.

I think that is why we believe that love has the power to last forever. Nothing else will satisfy us. Nothing else will do.

Long ago, Paul wrote a letter to a church in Corinth, Greece. His words aimed at bringing people closer together to teach them the true meaning of life. These words have been read at thousands of weddings. They have lifted the souls of the sorrowful. They have moved millions. And the words themselves still have the power to make love fresh.

> *If I speak in the tongues of mortals and of angels, but do not have love, I am a noisy gong or a clanging cymbal. And if I have prophetic powers, and understand all mysteries, and all knowledge, and if I have all faith, so as to remove mountains, but do not have love, I am nothing. If I give away all my possessions, and if I hand over my body to be burned, but do not have love, I gain nothing.*
>
> *Love is patient; love is kind; love is not envious or boastful or arrogant or rude. It does not insist on its own way; it is not irritable or resentful; it does not rejoice in wrongdoing, but rejoices in the truth. It bears all things, believes all things, hopes all things, endures all things.*
>
> *Love never ends. . . .*
>
> *And now faith, hope and love abide, these three; and the greatest of these is love.*
>
> —1 Cor. 13:1-8, 13 NRSV

PART THREE

Our Daily Work

7

Personal Goals

Nothing can bring you peace but yourself.

—Ralph Waldo Emerson, *Self-Reliance*

In October 1997, Ana Molina Osorio graduated from high school. "So what?" you might say. Millions of people graduate from high school every year.

Maybe so, but not after being a dropout. And not at the age of 102.

Ana Molina, a great-great-grandmother, is still in love with life, even though she has had her share of hardships. When she was a child she was forced to hide in a shack when soldiers invaded her home in Puerto Rico. Later she was forced to drop out of school to support herself and her family. She went to work selling tickets in a silent-film theater.

But she never gave up on her goal of earning her high school diploma. It just took her longer than most. Each day, in addition to taking care of her family, and now her great-grandchildren and great-great-grandchildren, she wrote poetry and tried to inspire others, urging them to never give up on their goals. She was a good role model, for Ana Molina never abandoned her dream.

Neither should you or I. For without our dreams, our personal goals, life becomes too formidable and sterile. We need our dreams to keep us alive and to help us focus our energies.

The decade of the 1990s may well go down in American history as the decade of personal dreams and self-evaluation. Self-help gurus and personal-growth experts abound. Motivational speaking has become a big-time occupation, and millions of people are looking to find the keys of success in every avenue of life—whether it be financial, relational or spiritual. Every week our newspapers and televisions are filled with advertisements and seminars on how to be a more effective investor, a better parent, a better spouse, a better business partner or a more wholesome individual. Most bookstores even have self-help or personal-growth sections, where books of this nature can be found.

But why this great desire to be better individuals? What is it that drives us to desire new insights, to find the keys for living a good and happy life? Why do we want to constantly improve ourselves?

I think the answers to these questions can be found in the nature of life itself. Life is change. Life is a series of constant challenges. Our desire to be better than we were the day before stems from our hope for a better tomorrow. Now, that may be a very American attitude, but I think it is almost universally true.

We want to improve ourselves so that we can meet the challenges of tomorrow. Go to any country, talk to the people there, and I think you would discover that most are trying to better their lot in one way or another. People want to rise above their circumstances. Most everyone has personal goals, things they would like to achieve in life.

When I was a boy, I had some goals, but most of them centered on things like sports and recreation. I wanted to develop a better jump shot, a better baseball swing or catch a bigger fish. I really couldn't understand why some of my friends found such fascination in paper routes and serving up sodas at the local pharmacy. Even though they were earning money, the price they had to pay for lost time at the baseball diamond or after-school activities seemed to pale in comparison.

But all of this changed for me when I started mowing Mrs. Blair's lawn. Suddenly I was caught up in this thing called success, and I didn't want to fail at it.

Mrs. Blair was an elderly widow who had lived alone for more than twenty years. She occupied a small white house on the corner, three blocks down the street from where I grew up. During the summer of my sixteenth year, I began mowing her lawn with all the zest of a one-armed drunk. But Mrs. Blair would have nothing of it. She made it known right away that she expected far more from me than a quick scalping of her lawn.

"You're mowing the grass too short," she told me one afternoon. "And I prefer the wheel lines to run parallel to the sidewalk. And while you're at it, honey, get those weeds out of the flower bed."

Mrs. Blair was so sweet about it that I couldn't be angry with her. Instead, I worked all summer to achieve my ultimate

goal: making Mrs. Blair happy. I mowed the grass a bit higher
and walked parallel to the sidewalk. I trimmed around each
fence post and edged the sidewalk by hand until my knuckles
bled. I went to work on the flower garden filled with weeds.
I spread fertilizer. I swept the back porch with a broom.
Whenever I noticed a flaw, I attempted to fix it right away. I
wanted to make a good impression with my effort.

June and July passed and I was still getting Cs. By August I
had worked myself up to a B. Finally September rolled around
and I knew I had done all I could. Now it was in the Lord's
hands.

"You've done such a good job, honey," Mrs. Blair told me
one Saturday in early October. The trees were beginning to
turn gold and purple, and I had spent most of the morning
raking the fallen leaves into bags. "You're so conscientious,
honey," she continued. "Here's a little something extra for all
your good work." She handed me an extra dollar and I studied
it for several long seconds before folding it delicately and slip-
ping it into my pocket. That dollar tip was like the crown
jewel of success. I even thought about having it framed, but I
went down to the bait and tackle shop and bought a dozen
nightcrawlers instead.

Actually, it wasn't the money that mattered. It was the joy
of setting a goal and meeting it. Receiving that good word
from Mrs. Blair elevated me to a different level of personal
achievement. I knew there was no telling what I could
accomplish. Why, I might even make mayor.

In fact, that next summer I received a promotion and began
mowing the town cemetery. I mowed that chunk of real estate
for a couple of weeks (until I discovered the cemetery was

loaded with snakes and gave up the position for reasons of personal health). After that I dabbled in house painting and odd jobs, although my father ended up doing most of the painting (which was not odd at all). I was well into my twenties before I realized that my future resided in the academic world, and so I took to studying subjects like Greek and Latin and obscure Romantic poetry, knowing that, with subjects like these under my belt, I would be a highly marketable individual when I graduated from college.

Fortunately for me, I never gave up on this stuff; I just learned how to use it. I came to realize that personal goals are as much a matter of creativity and perspective as anything. One simply has to learn how to look.

Having a goal in life is important. Without goals, we just putter around, uncertain of our fate and future, uncertain of where we are heading. A clear goal is like a compass—it directs us and helps us navigate our way through all of life's possibilities. I've come to regard personal goals as tiny visions. The goals are out there; we just have to find them and believe in them.

Without imagination and desire, it is easy for us to get lost in the darkness. Having a goal is like steering a ship by way of the North Star. We have to focus on something bright and unwavering, or we may never reach our destination.

Everyone, I believe, has goals of one type or another. And, since we are all different, our goals will be slightly different as well.

Some people, for example, want to make loads of money. They set out to achieve financial success, and they never stop until they've made their first million. Other people regard success as having a solid marriage and a loving family. Some think of success in terms of personal happiness and friendship. Others want peace of mind and lots of privacy.

And then there is J. Irwin Miller.

The fact that you have probably never heard of the man should be no surprise, though his accomplishments and his company may be well known to many. J. Irwin Miller took over the helm of the family business—Cummins Engine Company—in 1934 and built it into a Fortune 500 corporation. He began with sixty employees and, at the time of his retirement years later, employed some twenty-five thousand workers, with offices in one hundred countries. He transformed his company from a family affair into an international corporation of over $6 billion in annual sales.

So much for his business achievements.

J. Irwin Miller, throughout his life, has been a down-to-earth fellow whose accomplishments are rivaled only by his humility and generosity. As a Christian and a firm believer in human rights, Miller helped to organize Reverend Martin Luther King Jr.'s 1963 civil rights march on Washington. He also gave millions of his own money to aid voter-registration drives throughout the South, and he was an opponent of the war in Vietnam during a time when such a stand was unthinkable for a man in his position. He also contributed millions of his personal fortune to local charities, churches and building projects in his native Hoosier state. But not one building, anywhere, bears a cornerstone, a plaque or a sign with his name on it.

Over his career, Miller has made it a goal to give away 30 percent of his pretax salary. And once, when it appeared that the company was going to be bought out by a hostile takeover bid, Miller and his sister used $65 million of their own money to purchase additional company stock, thwart the bid and secure their employees' jobs.

So much for his humanitarian achievements. In addition, Miller has had a successful and happy lifelong marriage. He has five children and ten grandchildren. This is what he counts as his greatest accomplishment. That and his great desire to love his neighbors, whom he defines as anyone he meets.

Miller was in combat for eighteen months in the South Pacific during World War II and, upon returning to the helm of his company, immediately put an end to the segregated workplace. When apartheid grew more resilient in South Africa, Miller closed his Cummins factory in South Africa as a means of protest. He lost millions of dollars, but he gained much more, as his decisions helped to free Nelson Mandela from prison after a twenty-seven-year political confinement.

Miller has known most of the American presidents from the time of Eisenhower, and his counsel has been sought by national and international leaders from both ends of the political spectrum, and points in between. From JFK to Nixon, from Carter to Reagan, from King to Mandela, J. Irwin Miller has been involved in some of the most important decisions and history-making moments of our time. But he has made a name for himself by not making a name for himself.

In a time when fame and self-aggrandizement are the grandest of achievements, Miller has lived quietly in a southern Indiana town, surrounded by familiar faces and voices, at peace with the world and, most importantly, with himself and his Maker. Although he has received numerous awards and certificates of recognition throughout his life, he displays none of these in his office. Rather, they gather dust in the closet. Miller is a plain man in an age of glitz and glitter and self-promotion.

These days, Miller, age eighty-nine, isn't as active as he used to be. He has pared his personal goals back a bit. Now he spends his time teaching himself Italian and reading histories of the Roman Empire in preparation for trips overseas. He loves being a husband, father and grandparent. He enjoys reading the classics. Mostly, he just wants to be a good neighbor.

So much for his life.

You think folks like J. Irwin Miller are rare? Not according to him. All a person needs to be successful, to reach one's personal goals, is a heart of love, the desire to find a human need, and the faith and fortitude to see a solution through to the end. He doesn't count his success in terms of dollars and cents, but in terms of how much joy and hope he has been able to give away during his lifetime.

How much of that spirit do you and I possess? Are these the kinds of personal goals we strive for? I hope so.

On a far different front, there are other people who inspire me with their simplicity and matchless wonder at the world around them. Their goals may not make the morning headlines, but they are powerful testimonies of the human spirit.

First let me tell you about Barbara, a woman who had lived with her father all of her life but, after her father's death, was forced to move into a facility staffed with nurses and round-the-clock care. Although Barbara was confined to a wheelchair, she could do most things for herself, and the adjustment, at first, was difficult. Her initial weeks in this new place were depressing and defeating. But Barbara persevered.

One afternoon, during a visit, I noted that Barbara had a new addition to her room—a personal computer. I asked her about it.

"I'm on the Internet," she told me. "I'm going to see the world."

That was one of the most inspiring statements I'd heard in a long time. Barbara could have given up on life, but instead, at age sixty, she chose to embrace the future with a new goal: seeing the world through her personal computer. The fact that she had never owned a computer before wasn't going to stop her. Her personal loss and her less-than-perfect living situation were not going to get in her way. She decided to make a future for herself. By golly, she was on the Net!

Or take the little chap I met one afternoon in a small Canadian town. I was working with teenagers during our annual summer mission trip when he rode up on a bicycle, dismounted and ran over to join our group. We were sitting in a field, playing games with a large parachute, and he was spellbound.

"Where did you get this parachute?" he asked. "Whose is it? How do you play? Where are you from? Do you care if I play, too?" On and on he went, asking one question after another.

Finally, after he had played for a while, he came over to me, puffed up his chest, and announced that someday he was going to jump out of an airplane and parachute safely to earth.

"When are you going to do it?" I asked him.

He thought for a moment. "Before I am twenty-one," he said smartly.

A small goal, but then a lot of bigger dreams are composed of smaller goals, aren't they? Isn't this how Edison and the Wright Brothers went about their business of dreaming big dreams and working to make them a reality?

Every day I meet people who are striving to reach one goal or another. How about the many Boy Scouts who are working to earn merit badges or to achieve the rank of Eagle Scout? The men and women who are taking the risk, and following their dream, of owning and operating their own business? Or how about the individuals whose goals are more eclectic, people who want to climb mountains, or sail seas, or work on a space mission to Mars?

What are your goals in life? What keeps you going and growing?

As I've tried to answer these questions for myself, I keep going back to something I once heard in a college classroom years ago. I was taking a freshman English class, studying sentence structure and composition and all manner of things parsed and participled, when one student raised his hand and asked the professor a tantalizing freshman question: "What difference does any of this make?"

The professor, a shrunken little man with a soft voice and a bow tie, meekly descended from his podium and faced the student as if he were about to draw a six-shooter. He cleared his throat and said, "Some things make a difference because they can make *us* different. I only hope that, somewhere along the line, while you are a student in this institution of higher learning, you will learn that investing in yourself, in your mind and experiences and understanding of the world around you, is the best investment you can make."

I've never forgotten those words, and I do believe that investing in ourselves is, indeed, the best investment we can make. That's what personal goals are all about. That's why the striving and the aching and the hoping are so important. Without the desire, we'd just shrivel and die.

Our personal goals, however, need not be identified with great achievements to bring us fulfillment. For some, achieving success and obtaining wealth only brings anguish and heartache. Rather than being a source of joy, such success might prove to be a source of unhappiness for many.

Likewise, the little goals we set for ourselves on a daily basis might prove to be more fulfilling and stirring than any of life's larger accomplishments. Spending a day in the yard or preparing a Thanksgiving dinner for the entire family might be as joyous an accomplishment as could be imagined. In this manner, each day can present its own challenges and goals.

Or, to put it another way, success is in the eye of the beholder. Setting our sights on the highest accomplishments may well mean taking the lowest road, the path of service and devotion to others. Or it may mean that we have found our own source of happiness and have discovered that the simple things, like enjoying a sunset or spending a day with friends, are sufficient unto themselves.

In essence, the goals we set for ourselves are entirely of our own making. No one can make them for us. And that is precisely why they are personal.

With that thought in mind, I leave you with this final story.

A wealthy businessman went on vacation. One day he was getting ready to rent a boat when he happened to notice a fisherman lying in the sun, calmly smoking his pipe.

"Why aren't you out there on the lake today?" the businessman asked. "This is a great day to be catching fish."

"I've already caught enough fish today," the fisherman replied.

"Well, why don't you catch more?"

"What would I do with more?"

The businessman, always thinking about how to turn a profit and be successful, answered, "You could sell your extra fish in the market, and then you'd have enough money to rig up your boat with an outboard motor. Then you could go out into the deeper waters and catch even more fish. After a time, you'd have enough money to buy nets. Then you could really start making a business for yourself. You could buy another boat, hire a crew of fisherman to work for you, maybe even get a fleet of fishing boats. You'd be a rich man in no time."

"And what would I do then?" the fisherman wanted to know.

"Then you could sit back, smoke your pipe and really enjoy life," the businessman answered.

"Well," the fisherman said, "what do you think I'm doing right now?"

8

Meaningful Work

Whatever your hand finds to do,
do with your might.

—Eccles. 9:10 NRSV

In the spring of 1990, I received a postcard informing me
that Miss Maudy had died at the age of 104 and that, in
accordance with her lifelong wishes, she had been buried in
the cemetery outside the Fair Promise Church in Bear Creek,
North Carolina. This news did not particularly surprise me,
for Miss Maudy had been ailing for years. But I had long held
to the hope that she might go on forever.

Miss Maudy had lived a lifetime with her brother, Mr.
Jesse (age 102), in a refurbished log cabin, which their father
had built prior to the Civil War. The house—erected on a
slouching foundation during an era when bricks and mortar
were a scarce commodity—was replete with odd angles and

dimensions, no room meeting in perpendicular lines. The walls and ceiling seemed to merge together in a disjointed battle of plaster and exposed studs. The panes of glass inside the windows were wavy and bubbly as circus mirrors, and the floor was a myriad of bumps and warps.

Every month, for nearly two years, I visited Miss Maudy and Mr. Jesse in their home, listened to their stories of the olden times, and learned the value and meaning of work.

Miss Maudy, known for her made-from-scratch pound cake, baked a fresh batch every Monday morning: a large wheel of the pastry centered on the countertop in the kitchen, a few slices covered with wax paper, awaiting any unexpected guests. She made freshly squeezed lemonade sweetened with sugar. Afternoons and evenings she sat on the threadbare couch in the tiny living room, working on a quilt or a doily.

Mr. Jesse, her brother, found it difficult to give up his chores, even in the heat of August. He mowed the yard, tended a vegetable garden and tinkered in the woodshed, often turning table legs on a lathe. His aged hands were like leather, veins running along his forearms like a map of rivers, palms callused like stone.

I remember them this way because that is how they would have wanted it—this brother and sister who had spent a lifetime together, who had worked side by side for nearly a century. I remember them this way because they found meaning in their work. Their lives were as intricately intertwined in life as they would be in death.

Even so, they were delightful in their idiosyncrasies, for Miss Maudy and Mr. Jesse loved to argue.

Often, in the afternoon, Mr. Jesse would pop in a huge chew of tobacco, sit down at his rolltop desk and tune in the Atlanta Braves on his ancient Philco radio. Miss Maudy, stitching a quilt, would make the mistake of asking a question during this sacred hour. And the arguing would commence. A person standing outside the house could not miss the commotion, for each needed to shout louder than the other in order to be heard—especially if Miss Maudy turned off her hearing aid.

This, too, I suppose, was a portion of their work on earth— to torment each other as brothers and sisters often do.

They could never agree, in part because Miss Maudy had a stubborn streak in her that ran all the way up her spine and down again to her feet. She never gave up on anything, not even attending church.

Every week Miss Maudy would occupy her usual pew: second from the front on the right-hand side near the pulpit. She inevitably arrived early to make certain that no one took her seat. She sang the hymns with gusto, said the prayers. But, every Sunday, about halfway through the worship service, Miss Maudy would have what she called "a spell." She would faint away into the center aisle—just keel over like a domino. No one batted an eye.

Miss Maudy had been having spells in church for as long as most folks could remember. They were used to it. Two or three ushers would walk casually up the aisle, take Miss Maudy by the arms or legs and carry her out to a car. One of the ushers would drive her home.

The next Sunday Miss Maudy would be right back at it, spell and all. With her it was always two hymns and out! She never did get to stay long enough to hear one of my sermons. Many suspected that this was her way of protesting against preachers.

I don't know, but I wish she could have been around long enough to hear all of the nice things I actually said about her. I did love her.

Equally deep as her stubbornness was her sense of hospitality. Every person who ever visited Miss Maudy had to eat a piece of pound cake and drink a glass of lemonade. No exceptions. And, upon departure, she always wrapped a second piece of pound cake in a sheet of waxed paper. I guess she wanted folks to remember her at home, too.

There was one visit that was particularly memorable for me. As soon as I walked in the door, Miss Maudy demonstrated her hospitality by bringing me a piece of pound cake and a glass of lemonade. We sat for a time, visiting with Mr. Jesse, talking of things long since passed, and it was then that I noticed a decrepit shack nestled on the hillside beyond the house. It stood among evergreens and bald kudzu vines, a slouching edifice that had seen the better part of a century and was now being eaten away by age and water rot. The shack, for want of a better word, looked important in its deterioration, and I asked Mr. Jesse about it.

Turning off the radio, he pivoted in the chair near his rolltop and pointed toward the hill. "That's the old wood shop," he told me. "That's where Maud and I worked . . . back when we was in our prime."

"What did you do up there?"

"We made caskets," he informed me.

"Caskets?"

Mr. Jesse sat down next to Miss Maudy and rummaged through his mind for the proper words. "It's got quite a life," he said, "that old shed up there. Maud and I started turning out caskets before the depression. Back then, we made the finest caskets around. People come from miles over to buy 'em."

"You're too young to remember," Miss Maudy informed me. "But there weren't no funeral parlors in them days. When someone died, we went out to the home and measured the body. Made a custom casket to fit the dead. Back then, people had wakes in their homes, and everyone dropped by to view the body, bring food and pay their last respects. When the wake was over, the circuit preacher come by and said words for a proper burial."

"I made the caskets," Mr. Jesse interjected. "Usually oak or cherry, sometimes pine or maple. Maud, she done the inside of the caskets—made the padding, embroidered the pillows, done all the fancy ruffles and lace for the ladies, made something simple for the men."

The scent of winter pine wafted through the cracked windows, and I peered out at the evergreens laced with hoarfrost. "You made caskets—right there in that shed?" I asked.

"The *best*," Miss Maudy replied. "That is . . . until the depression."

"What happened then?"

"Folks was dirt poor in them days," Mr. Jesse said. "Couldn't afford to buy a scrap of lumber. So, instead of making the best caskets, we made the cheapest. That way folks could still buy 'em. During the depression, them caskets was little more than pine boxes."

I realized I was talking to a couple of shrewd business tycoons. "So you made the best caskets when times were good and the least expensive when times were bad."

Mr. Jesse nodded, his hands rough hewn as timbers. "It's a good work," he told me. "And it's been a good life. We ain't highfalutin folks, but it's a good life."

A good work. And a good life.

Yes, I can believe that. So can you.

Meaningful work doesn't have to pay well (though that's a plus), and it doesn't have to be prestigious or sophisticated to make us feel good about ourselves and others. In fact, I'm convinced that meaningful work is more of an attitude than an aptitude. I've met unhappy millionaires and giddy gas station attendants, depressed oil tycoons and smiling waitresses. Money doesn't make for happiness in a job; and the most difficult jobs can often bring out character and integrity in people.

The newspapers are full of stories about professional athletes who dread the very thought of playing another game for a measly million. We've all heard of the corporate CEO who makes big bucks, yet has a rotten marriage, drinks to excess or cannot earn the respect of his laborers. But no one writes about the millions of people who do their jobs day in and day out for far less pay, and yet find a purpose and meaning in their work.

One of life's greatest blessings, I'm convinced, is the ability to find joy and pleasure in our daily efforts. This is a commodity that cannot be sold to the highest bidder.

Over the years, however, I've met many people who despise what they do. They seem unfulfilled, unhappy. They often see their occupations as mere jobs to be performed, sheer drudgery taken to the limits of boredom.

Is there any remedy to this? Is it possible to find meaningful work?

I think so. At least . . . I have observed that it is so.

When I was a boy I knew a man named Penny who lived down the street from our house. No one seemed to know exactly what Penny did for a living, and there were more than a few people in town who thought that Penny was half a brick shy of a full load. Yet, in all my encounters with Penny, I cannot recall a single instance when he was not smiling.

He gathered junk from the local landfill, collected aluminum cans along the roads and scavenged for iron spikes along the railroad tracks. He didn't own much, but he always had time to fish, and hunt, and gather walnuts and flowers. Many were the days when I saw him emerging from our woods with a brimming pail of summer blackberries. I knew that he took them into town and sold them, but he never failed to offer me a few berries to keep his secret.

Since that time, I've grown to consider myself a competent interpreter of the human spirit. I've found that I can discern a good deal about a man or woman just by watching him or her at work. I can tell by the way someone sits at a desk, or holds a pencil, or types at a keyboard whether that individual has found significance in his or her labor. Fulfillment is found in the nuances, all the little things that make a job more than just a job. It is found in the way someone greets a coworker in the morning, the way a person gives a presentation, the manner in which a person deals with conflict and seeks to find peaceful and productive resolutions. The best and happiest workers find meaning in the journey itself, in the giving of the self, rather than in the receiving of a paycheck.

Often, when I meet people and the conversation turns from one subject to another, as small talk inevitably does, the subject of work usually rises to the top. Especially with men. We are fascinated with work, and we want to know what another fellow does for a living. I suppose men find this type of comparison competitive. Usually, it's the jobs with the biggest bucks that get the most respect.

But sometimes, I like to ask: "Why do you do what you do?"

Some folks give the strangest answers. Some shoot back trite phrases or bitter credos. Some wax philosophical about the stock market and the joys of having a top-notch 401(k). Others can't answer at all.

But one fellow dredged up this uncommon answer: "I'm in competition with myself." I had met him at a wedding reception, an athletic type named Jerry, who happened to run a food-catering business. I asked him what he meant by this.

"The way I see it," he said, "I don't have to be better than anyone else. The only guy I have to top is me. I approach every day as an opportunity to make my business a little bit finer than it was the day before. That way, I don't worry about the other guy. I just worry about me, making myself better, doing a better job for my customers. And if I mess up, I don't lose sleep. I'm not perfect. Tomorrow is another day. It's like having a brand new at bat. No balls. No strikes. And I'm back to batting one thousand."

I have a feeling that Jerry not only likes his work, but he excels at it. He probably has one of the best catering businesses around.

People who like their work are generally more jovial and helpful as well. They go out of their way to please. They seem more caring.

Not long ago I experienced this reality firsthand when I went shopping for a certain type of wood screw. I visited a gigantic hardware store that sold every type of nut and bolt imaginable. But I still couldn't find what I was looking for. So I asked one of the floor clerks for assistance. The young lady gave me a sour look, as if to say, "How stupid are you, really, and why are you wasting my time?" She pointed to one corner of the store (a football field's distance away), mumbled a few words and then disappeared behind a wall of paint cans.

I departed, too, and went to a smaller hardware store on the other side of town.

Same problem, however. I couldn't locate what I needed among the selection of items. Disgusted with myself, I was about to leave empty handed when a young floor clerk approached and asked, "Can I help you with something?"

That made my day.

But I went home and thought about those two experiences, and those two employees—as different as night and day. I considered how I felt in each instance, and why. And I came to the conclusion that the only difference between the two floor clerks was in the attitude displayed by each. One had found meaningful work among the nuts and bolts. The other was simply doing a job.

There is a huge difference.

God save us from such drudgery. No one should have to do a job. But everyone should have a job to do.

Where are you in relationship to your work? Are you

fulfilled, or fed up? Are you on top of the world, or does it feel like the world is on top of you? Are you putting in time, or are you doing timely work?

I've spent a fair amount of my life talking with people about the meaning of it all. And, inevitably, this spans the significance of what we do each day. People want to do something, I'm convinced, that matters to others. They want to know that they are making a difference to someone, somewhere.

For this reason, I've always told people to trust their tingles when it comes to work. You have to go by the heart, by that deep-down gut feeling. What do you really want to do? Where do you find fulfillment? Where are you gifted? What are your talents and abilities?

Growing up, I was blessed to know a gentleman named Spike. Spike was the custodian at my grade school—a tall, lanky fellow with coal-blackened hands and a greasy smile. But the essence of his life was not defined by his job.

To all the boys at my school, Spike was something of an anomaly, a larger-than-life character who told us apocryphal tales about playing baseball with Ty Cobb and about how he had once pitched in the big leagues for half a season before his shoulder blew out and ended his promising career. Spike taught us how to throw a curve ball; he umpired our softball games; he gave us candy before lunch; he even let us shovel coal into the chute that stoked the monstrous iron furnace in the basement.

Spike knew how to transform a job that was often dirty and smelly into something quite beautiful and meaningful. In fact, I'm sure the administration often frowned upon his activity and interaction with us children. Perhaps he didn't keep the school warm enough in the winter or cool enough in the summer, but he kept his soul in the right place. He knew who he was. He did not allow his work to define the essence of his being. But, rather, he brought the essence of his being to his work.

His official title was custodian. But deep down he knew he was Spike—a big league pitcher who had once shared a base-ball field with Ty Cobb—a man who needed to pass on what he knew to a few children he loved.

If you find that you are in a dead-end job, or are just going through the motions in order to put food on your table or keep clothes on your children's back—don't despair. Look for the center of what you do and put something of yourself into your labor. But don't let your job define *you*. Rather, seek to transform your job hour by hour, day by day. Try to find those aspects of your work that bring pleasure and fulfillment— even if it means you have to create your own definition, or dream your own dream, or make up a few of your own rules. And by and by, you will discover that not only have you transformed your job, you have transformed yourself as well.

Or, if you like, take a lesson from Olivia Harris—a dear lady who lived the last seven years of her life confined to a bed, hands gnarled with arthritis, each breath a voluntary labor of the diaphragm. But still at work. Still with a job to do.

In spite of her condition, she never ceased to make get-well cards for others: handmade wonders, colorful and shaky as a child's first effort, but hers nonetheless. I came by every week to collect the cards for my regular hospital visits—these get-well wishes from a lady who had a great deal more "get-ting well" to do than most of the people I visited.

"*Why* do you do it?" I asked her each week. "*How* do you do it?"

Her answer was always the same: "Doing for others takes my mind off myself and my own misery. If I can't work for others, if I can't do for others, if I can't make a contribution, however small . . . well, that's the day I'll just roll up and die!"

This she offered to me each week, along with a prayer—a homespun prayer shot through with powerful words that made my spine tingle and my hair stand on end—a prayer for me. "Give him a work to do," she'd pray, as if I needed more work. "And give him the wisdom to know when to lie down and rest."

Yes, rest. The ability to know when work is done, when all things have been gathered into their proper places. This, too, is a part of meaningful work. Labor was never meant to be a life-consuming affair.

If we have learned anything about time, however, and about ourselves, we know that we have fallen prey to the delusion that more is better, to the belief that having the most things is the measure of life's meaning and work's greatest end. But, deep down, we know this is not so. It is the desire to be useful, to be needed, that drives even the most intense among us. The problem is, we don't often know how to channel these energies into the most useful of purposes, how to give back in the same measure that we have received, how to enjoy the very things we have worked so hard and long to obtain.

When all is said and done, the one with the most toys hasn't won anything at all. But the one who has lived long and well through his or her work will have gained the world and so much more: respect of family and friends, appreciation, the gift of love, the admiration of those who follow after.

There is a wonderful story about John D. Rockefeller, probably apocryphal in nature as most billionaire stories are. It seems that when Mr. Rockefeller died, there was great speculation about how much John D. was worth. Many wanted to know how his vast fortune would be divided. Many hoped that John D. would leave his wealth to various charities or philanthropic organizations. Tension mounted as the hours wore on. But eventually Mr. Rockefeller's lawyers appeared to answer questions.

Dozens of reporters and photographers converged on the scene. Flash bulbs popped. A reporter blurted out, "Tell us! What did Mr. Rockefeller leave? What did he leave?"

One of the lawyers calmly stepped forward to answer the question. "Why, Mr. Rockefeller left everything!"

Certainly. How is it possible to take anything with us?

Life itself has a way of teaching us such lessons. And there are many stories that remind us of the fleeting nature of life and the joys of self-giving labor. One might consider the lessons of the tranquil Buddha, the wise admonitions of Confucius or the parables of Jesus. There is far more to one's labors than acquiring things.

Among the vast collection of Jewish wisdom, the ancient rabbis told the parable of a man who had a wife and seven children. Each day this man would go fishing in order to provide food for himself and his family. And each day, without fail, and no matter how hard he tried otherwise, he would catch exactly nine fish—just enough for each person in the family to enjoy a single helping. But, as time went by, the fellow began to wish for more. "Why," he wondered, "do I always catch nine fish? Why can't I catch ten? Then I would be able to enjoy a second helping." For several months the man thought long and hard about this extra helping. He dreamed of the day when he would catch ten fish.

One day a messenger arrived with bad news: "Your youngest son has been killed in the field." All day long the man mourned the loss of his son, but, the next morning, the man's spirits were brightened with the prospect of having an extra fish to eat. "I will miss my son," the man thought, "but at least I will have an extra helping."

That day the man caught only eight fish—and no matter how hard he tried, he could not catch a ninth.

I don't know what centuries of interpretation and exegesis have done with this parable, but I do understand the essence of what it says about my life and yours. Our work is a blessing—if it gives meaning and provides for the common good. One doesn't have to earn more to find the center of meaningful work. Having what we need is a far greater blessing than wanting what we do not have.

Sometimes our work is best appreciated when we have done all we could, in spite of the fact that there is always more work to do. We will never exhaust the possibilities of life. Not even all the possibilities for meaningful labor.

I know this reality was true of Miss Maudy and Mr. Jesse. They had learned that work is something we give each day. And good work is free.

My last visit with Miss Maudy and Mr. Jesse was something of an affirmation of this spirit, as I was given a gift that I cherish to this day. My wife (then my fiancée) had come with me to visit the aging brother and sister on a summer day, not long before our wedding day. She had listened to my tales about Miss Maudy and Mr. Jesse with reserved skepticism, certain that I was embellishing on a point or two along the way.

But she discovered what I had known all along—that here were two genuine people who had learned the art of labor as no others.

On that summer day we entered the heirloom cabin, passed through a narrow hallway where Mr. Jesse's muzzle-loader hung on a parched wall and sat down on dusty furnishings. Miss Maudy was quick to bring us each a piece of pound cake (freshly baked that morning) and a glass of lemonade. Mr. Jesse turned off the Philco radio and gazed out, proudly, at the manicured lawn he had just finished mowing.

Then, with no haste, and no want of anything at all, we sat for a spell and talked about nothing that mattered much. And all was right with the world.

At last, after some time that filled less than a day and more than an afternoon, my wife-to-be and I rose from our chairs to take our final leave.

"Wait right there," Miss Maudy directed us. "I've got a wedding gift for you both."

Becky and I watched as Miss Maudy disappeared into the bedroom and returned carrying a multicolored quilt, a creation of scraps and patches that she had sewn together with trembling hands at the age of 101. She gave the quilt away in the same charitable spirit in which she had sewn it, a humble gesture of her own uniqueness and practicality.

"I know it ain't purty," she told us. "It ain't highfalutin. But I made it, and it'll keep you warm."

That afternoon we left with Miss Maudy's quilt, and we have it to this day. True to her word, that quilt has kept us warm, not so much through winter nights as through moments of crisis and uncertainty, when all the world seemed cold and lonely and distant. That quilt has kept us safe and warm in the knowledge that Miss Maudy's and Mr. Jesse's life together was something of a labor of love.

It was a few years later that I received word that Miss Maudy had passed away at the age of 104. She was buried beside the Fair Promise United Methodist Church, not far from the pew where she had her spells. I'm sure she wanted it that way.

Only a few days later I learned that Mr. Jesse had joined her. Dead at the age of 101. Some said that when Miss Maudy went, Mr. Jesse wilted like a flower and faded. Their lives had been so intertwined that there was no way one could live without the other. In the same manner as they had lived, they died.

I have long wondered what I would say to Miss Maudy and Mr. Jesse if I could see them again, if I could sum up the significance of their labors and make it plain, if I could give back to them a little of what they have given to me. And I have come to the conclusion that I would say it in a way they could understand, in simple words that would leave them smiling with delight and in awe of what they had accomplished. They are words we would all like to hear at the end of our days:

Miss Maudy, Mr. Jesse, you done good. No, you didn't live too purty, nor too highfalutin. But you done good. A lot of good. And we thank you.

9

Inspired Volunteerism

Give your services for nothing. . . .
And if there be an opportunity of serving one
who is a stranger, give full assistance.

—Hippocrates

The morning star, Venus, shone brilliantly in the Mediterranean sky as the bus bounced along the darkened roads leading out of Jerusalem. I looked up and down the center aisle of the bus at the other weary volunteers who swayed back and forth in their seats each time the bus dipped and turned. I checked my watch. It was not yet 5:00 A.M.

Ahead of me sat two women from Australia. To their left, three young men from Germany conversed in thick gutturals. Near the front of the bus, a cadre of students from Canada checked their equipment: shovels, work gloves, picks and brushes. Immediately behind me sat a woman who had lived in Israel during the Six-Day War. A younger Israeli talked softly with one of the guides. To my left sat an Islamic student from the States, head tilted back, mouth open in anticipation of a snore.

Up and down the bus I noted others—a few people from European countries, a woman from Great Britain, many from the United States. Together we rode the jolting bus into the Israeli countryside, the cool morning air splashing across our faces, all wondering what we had gotten ourselves into.

We were archaeological volunteers, eager to get at the stuff of history—dirt and stone and brick. We had come from points around the world, ready to contribute to the cause of self-discovery and the unearthing of human history. In those early morning hours, we gave no consideration to our differences of nationality, religion or creed. We were bound together in a common quest.

When the bus edged off the main road and tilted gingerly to one side, everyone roused and caught the first glimpse of sunrise. Our driver ground the gears until the cogs caught and the bus lurched forward. Anxiously we craned our necks to see what was over the crest of the hill, but the bus came to an abrupt stop as our guide jumped out.

A flurry of activity followed as we loaded picks and shovels into wheelbarrows, and began the trek up the narrow path leading to the ancient city of Beth Shemesh. We arrived at the site as the first pink fingers of dawn stretched across the valley. Lights from smaller hamlets on the hillsides flickered in the morning mist.

Barking instructions in English and Hebrew, the archaeologists moved the group to one side of the hill, where we began our dig. The entire area had been partitioned into grids—deepening squares separated by a narrow bulk, some two feet wide. We worked in teams, each assigned to a particular grid for the duration of the dig.

That first day, as morning lengthened and the fog lifted from the grasses, we began to note each other for the first time. We saw faces, nationalities. Heard the different dialects and languages. We took mental notes of who was Jew and Gentile, Christian and Muslim. But nothing mattered except the scattering of stones and the hauling of dirt. We celebrated each time we hit upon the discovery of broken pottery shards or chipped stone tools.

Across the valley, we saw the stark realities of the political and religious hatreds. A huge section of wheat field had been burned during the night by the Intifada—the Palestinian resistance, which had laid siege to the countryside. A gaping square of charred chaff reminded us that, although we were bound together on one small hill, the world beyond was still at war.

The spirit of volunteerism in that torn land affected us all. We sat at a table together for breakfast and lunch, talked of common joys, shared pictures of family and friends we missed back home (wherever home happened to be), and encouraged each other with stories of archaeological discoveries and the hopes of finding something special among the ruins of Beth Shemesh. Some vowed to keep in touch after the dig. Others became good friends.

That archaeological dig on a hillside in Israel was the first time I had seen so many people from so many countries working side by side without reservation. It was the first time

I had seen Jew, Christian and Muslim bound together in a common goal.

When we journeyed into Jerusalem together, we were turned back at the bus stop, where a soldier informed us that someone had planted a bomb on a bus. But we remained together. We seemed to cling to the hope that people could learn to live in peace.

And to think that a mound of dirt and some bits of broken pottery had made this possible. . . .

The spirit of volunteerism is universal. This spirit runs through the heart and asks us to turn aside from our individual pursuits to give some time to others, or to a common goal. Every day we have opportunities to make something greater of our communities and nation.

There is no doubt that, without the work of volunteers, everything you and I enjoy would be more difficult and far more expensive. Take hospitals for instance. How many times have you checked on a patient's room number at the reception desk in the lobby or talked with the receptionist in the surgery waiting room? Chances are, you talked with a volunteer. Someone gave their time out of the goodness of the heart, and not for the reward of a paycheck. Health care costs are high now. But can you imagine how much higher those costs would be without the thousands of volunteers who give their time to our hospitals and other health care facilities?

Or take the thousands of community agencies and services you and I enjoy each day—most of which we never stop to think about. Many public schools rely upon volunteer helpers to assist teachers. And what about Little League coaches?

Scout leaders? People who keep booths open at the state and county fairs? Volunteer fire departments? Crime watch groups? Library sponsors?

Or what about all the volunteers who take a section of highway and agree to keep it clean? Or those who plant flowers in city parks or along the curbside? Have you ever noticed how many people volunteer their time to various foundations, charities and fund-raising efforts across the country? The list could go on and on.

The thing is, although we enjoy the benefits derived from other volunteers, we often downplay the importance of being a volunteer ourselves. A great many things in this world simply wouldn't get done if not for the willingness of the few to make things possible for the many. Sometimes we start at the wrong end of the spectrum, wanting to know what we can get for free or for next to nothing. But the spirit of volunteerism begins at the point of seeing a need, looking to give rather than to receive.

John F. Kennedy once told the American people, "Ask not what your country can do for you. Ask what you can do for your country." This is at the heart of what it means to be a good citizen, an active volunteer. In essence, we are desperately needed. Our work, our gifts, our time—all these make a difference to someone.

This truth hit home with me a few years ago when some folks in my community circulated the idea that we needed to organize a local chapter of Habitat for Humanity. Although this county was the most affluent in the state, and one of the most affluent in the Midwest, many people in the area could not afford adequate housing. Because real estate prices were so high, few families (even on two incomes) could afford to purchase a home. Many rented apartments, houses and mobile homes for exorbitant sums, although in many instances the conditions were deplorable.

I'm convinced that Habitat for Humanity is one of the finest organizations in the world for bringing folks together under the banner of love. The people who showed up to help organize that chapter of Habitat came from all walks of life and from every point on the economic spectrum. That's one of the goals of Habitat: to bring communities closer together, to teach neighbors how to help neighbors. But the major goal is to eradicate substandard housing and to give every family a warm, dry and affordable home in which to live. Habitat brings a holistic approach to the problem of poverty.

Although I never pounded many nails or painted any walls for those initial Habitat projects, I spent a great deal of time helping with the people end of things. I interviewed prospective families, helped to provide emotional and community support for those who were selected to receive a Habitat home. Most of all, I tried to be a friend to those who needed a friend.

This effort demanded considerable energy and time from a multitude of people. But I saw the community coming together to make a difference for others. I was amazed at the range of talents and abilities people offered to the cause.

One of the most inspiring volunteers was an older woman who turned out to be the first recipient of a Habitat home. When I first met Belle, she was living alone in a tar-paper house on the outskirts of town. She was a widow who had raised several children in the home without the benefit of indoor plumbing, adequate heating or running water. But her positive spirit and attitude were infectious. She loved and loved and loved.

When I showed up at her door for the interview, I was amazed to find that I could not stand erect inside her home. The ceiling was only six feet above the floor, and because of this I was forced to stoop over. She told me her life story and how a friend had urged her to apply for a Habitat home. But I don't think she ever dreamed she would be the first one chosen to receive a home.

The day that Belle moved into her home was a time of celebration for many people: those who had volunteered their labors to build the home; those who had done the necessary legal work; those who had prepared food and organized fund-raisers and worked with the city council. Belle herself had invested her own sweat and tears in the endeavor, which is part of the wonder of Habitat for Humanity. In a sense, she had built her own home with the help of the community.

Belle moved out of a place that was cold and damp into a home that was warm and dry, surrounded by a community that loved her. But more than that, she gained a world of friendship and a new life. Inspired volunteerism happens whenever and wherever people work together to make a difference. And better yet, something happens in the human heart when we give ourselves to others.

This spirit of volunteerism is infectious. Perhaps this is because great friendships are discovered when people work side by side. It's tough for neighbors to hate each other when they are serving others. I have seen many instances of people putting aside differences to work together in a common cause.

Being a volunteer can be one of the most rewarding aspects of life. I think this is so because at the heart of every individual beats the desire to give. Giving reminds us that we are needed, that we are valued.

Most of us, for example, would be despondent if someone told us outright, "You are not needed." We might also feel angry and hurt. But to receive the call, to be asked to participate in an effort, to hear the words, "We really need you!"— such affirmations help us realize that others truly desire our talents. We have something to contribute, however small, that can make a difference to others.

When I consider my own history, I realize I have been a recipient of many volunteer hours. My Little League coaches were volunteers, as were the umpires—even though they had to endure the wrath of parents and fans. The same holds true for all the wonderful coaches who taught me how to dribble, pass and shoot a basketball. Although most were teachers, I know they weren't paid much to give so many extra hours to a motley crew of kids. I think about all those parents who helped with parties and proms, homecomings and dances. They gave. I know I'll need to do the same someday for my kids.

The spirit of volunteerism is not, however, reserved for adults. Children can learn to give. So can teenagers. The sooner the better.

My daughter attends a school where the children are encouraged to volunteer their time and talents to a variety of projects. Some children might agree to stay after school and help tutor younger children who are having problems with reading or mathematics. Others might give their time to a canned food drive for a local shelter. Some children have fun helping the teachers make bulletin boards or decorations for upcoming special days.

I have to think that this type of giving at an early age helps create a sense of self-worth and helps children to recognize their importance. Even children who are not performing well in school can find an outlet for their talents and abilities, a place to find affirmation and self-esteem. Being a volunteer can change the way children see themselves and can establish a lifelong pattern of giving to others.

I've also seen how this spirit of giving affects teenagers. Over the years I have helped organize many youth mission trips and, without exception, every teenager, I believe, was changed in some fashion by the experience of focusing upon others. And more than that, we always had a fun time in the process.

Soon after Hurricane Andrew swept across the Gulf and decimated parts of Florida, Georgia and other southern states, I found myself with a large group of teenagers who were helping to reconstruct the little town of Baldwin, Louisiana. Joe Mitchell, one of my best friends, had organized the trip. Over the years, we had taken many such trips together, and the teenagers always looked forward to these opportunities of service. Many returned year after year to give of themselves in this spirit of love and sharing.

In Louisiana, we not only endured the blistering summer heat, but we also worked to repair homes, assist with landscaping and help people whose homes had been ripped apart by the violent winds. Sometimes, when there were too many people and not enough work to go around, we simply visited with the residents. Often this kind of relaxed front-porch talk was every bit as important as painting a fence or hammering a nail. We were there to meet the needs of people, not just to repair homes.

I know that these teenagers, who are now young men and women, grew to count on their own abilities. They learned that they could give as well as receive. They found out from firsthand experience that life is not always easy, that there is much suffering in the world. But they also learned that they could help ease some portion of the world's sorrow and loss. That's volunteerism in its finest hour!

One unforgettable mission moment occurred in Dallas, Texas. We had traveled halfway across the country to discover that our living arrangements for the week were less than perfect. We were forced to sleep on the floor, crowded against each other like cordwood. We were forced to share two small bathrooms and a single shower.

Every day was a scorcher. It was difficult to sleep at night, and our weariness mounted as the week progressed. And yet the teenagers held up well under the stress—in fact, they held up much better than the adults.

In a two-day period, we completely scraped, sanded and painted one woman's home. We also worked in a soup kitchen and a homeless shelter. We sorted clothing at a Salvation Army center. But our main focus was always on the people. We made it a point to spend time with the people we were helping, being friends to them, being ourselves.

That particular summer I saw how teenagers have a gift for working with disadvantaged and troubled children. So many children look up to teenagers as role models, as big brothers and sisters. When they meet teenagers who really love and care for them, the encounters can be life-changing. I know that teenagers can make a difference in the lives of children. Providing these types of experiences can transform not only the children, but teenagers as well.

The spirit of volunteerism also compels us to be thankful. People who give of their time and talent usually appreciate the little things of life. They are out there on the edge, helping others, because they realize how much they have received from others.

I imagine the opposite is equally true. Folks who hoard their time and energy, focusing solely upon themselves, probably never stop to consider how much others have given to them. They may entertain the notion that they are self-sufficient, that they don't need others, but if they step out of the house and enter society, chances are they are going to cross paths with a volunteer sooner or later. Someone is giving to them, whether they realize it or not.

Giving something back is one of the ways we say thank you to the many who have added to our lives. We can't repay these people, but we can pass the goodness along by stretching out our hands and making an offering of our time. Volunteering is a kind of gift that keeps on giving.

When I was a kid, an elderly woman used to come around to our school each year to collect winter coats for children. In jest, we called her the Coat Lady. I don't even remember her name. She just showed up a few weeks before Christmas, made a speech about needy children and how cold it was going to be when the winter set in, and all of us seemed to convince our parents that we could make a contribution. It seemed that every year she walked out of the school with more coats than there were children.

But one year the Coat Lady didn't return. Someone else came in her place—a new, improved model—a younger woman with an hourglass figure. At least, the boys noticed the change.

This younger woman told us that the Coat Lady had died. She said she was taking up the mantle of service and would be collecting the winter coats that year. That was the first time I ever heard about taking up a mantle, and I wondered what it meant. It seems a mantle was some kind of a robe worn in ancient times, often passed from one servant to another as a kind of symbolic gesture of service. That image has always resonated in my mind. The Coat Lady died, but someone took her place.

When we serve well, we can rest assured that others are watching. Our service may well be an inspiration to others. Someone may even wish to be an apprentice, to be an under-study in the art of giving. Who's to say?

Many times I have seen volunteers who have burned out, or used themselves up in greater service to others, only to have someone else step in and take up the mantle. In a sense, this is exactly what Jesus and other great faith leaders managed to instill in their disciples. "There will come a day when I will no longer be with you," Jesus told his followers. "But you will do the works that I have done. You will take my place."

Being a volunteer is about following the examples of love and charity we have known from infancy. Other people fed and clothed us, taught us and encouraged us. A volunteer is someone who has not forgotten the good feeling that comes from receiving. And giving back feels even better. Or, as Jesus told his followers, "It is more blessed to give than to receive."

Becoming a great volunteer involves little more than

observing the world around us. What are the needs we see? Where are the gaps that need to be filled? Where can our talents and abilities best be used?

Yes, somebody needs us. Somebody can use what we have to give. Count on it.

Being a volunteer can also be a life-giving enterprise. Sometimes the service we render comes back to us in unexpected ways. We can give not only our time, but our money as well. We set out to help someone else but end up being the recipient of a greater good.

The story goes that, about a hundred years ago, an English boy was playing with some friends on a frozen pond when he broke through the ice and began to drown. Another boy named Fleming jumped in and saved his life. This memory lingered in the lad's mind and he never forgot what Fleming had done for him.

Years passed, friends parted and the lad (now a young man) continued to be haunted by the memory of the friend who had saved his life. One morning the young man set out to find his old friend and repay him for his bravery. He found Fleming in short order, thanked him for what he had done years ago and then offered him financial assistance. "My family is rather well off," he told Fleming, "and I would be happy to support you in a business endeavor or in some other dream you may have for your life."

Fleming was quick to point out that he had always dreamed of being of doctor, but had never had the means to attend a university. Soon thereafter, Fleming received word that he had been accepted into St. Mary's Medical School at the University of London and that his tuition was paid in full.

More years passed and Fleming not only graduated from medical school, but he began to make a name for himself through his research with green mold. Although Fleming's studies were well known in the medical community, the out-break of World War II relegated much of his research to the back pages of history. Meanwhile, the man who had once helped him get through medical school was making a name for himself on another front. Little did the two men know that their paths would cross again, though much later in life, at the crossroads of history.

In 1945, Alexander Fleming won the Nobel Prize for his discovery and development of penicillin—the life-saving antibiotic derived from green mold. This drug has no doubt saved thousands, probably millions, of lives.

But this is not the end of the story.

As World War II was winding down, the man who had volunteered to put Fleming through medical school became seriously ill with an infection. Word had it that the newly discovered drug, penicillin, could save his life. It did.

The man's name: Winston Churchill.

Winston Churchill was the man who had given and Alexander Fleming was the man who had received; although, in essence, Fleming saved Churchill's life not once, but twice! Think of it—had Churchill forgotten his friend, had he not volunteered to give his money for that college education—he would have been a diminished person without a spirit of giving, even though he was wealthy.

There is an old saying: The life you save may be your own. And in the case of Winston Churchill, this saying held true. Churchill's service, his gifts, his charity—these voluntary offerings—made a difference to the world not once, but twice: first through a man who discovered a wonder drug, and then again through the gift of his own life in service to his country.

Each of us has something to give to others, however large or small. Each of us can make a contribution to the good of society, in whole or in part, whether we are rich or poor.

Volunteering has nothing to do with making a name for ourselves, or earning great rewards; quite the opposite. These are the things we wish to give because they inspire and energize us, because they make us want to dance and sing.

At the heart of our giving stands a final elemental truth: We want to be remembered for good. When our name is spoken on the lips of others, we desire our name to be associated with the goodness and joy of life. We long to be remembered as one who gave back more than was received.

Walking through a cemetery one day, I came upon a tombstone epitaph that summarized this spirit well—these words that seemed to speak loudly for the one who rested from life's labors:

Gone But Not Forgotten
A True Servant
A Good Soul

Yes, that's how you and I want to be remembered, too.

PART FOUR

Moments to Treasure

10

Simple Pleasures

Consider not pleasures as they come,
but as they go.

—traditional proverb

In one corner of my office stands a set of bookshelves that are a story of simple pleasures.

Years ago, when I had graduated from seminary and taken my first appointment, my wife and I moved into a cracker box of a dwelling called a parsonage. The first time my wife saw the house, the entire back wall had been knocked down and we could look through the front door and see the corn-field behind. There was no carpeting on the floors, the cabinets in the kitchen had been ripped out and all the windows needed to be replaced. Furthermore, I had accumulated a sizable collection of books and had no place to put them. Because books are important to pastors (they make us look

intelligent—sitting there in rows like trophies to be adored),
I waited eagerly for the day when I could unbox and arrange
them neatly in a prominent place.

One of the first people I met in the new parish was a fellow named Herman. He was the church treasurer and,
because he signed my paycheck, I naturally took a liking to
him. Pastors never bite the hand that feeds them, and even if
a church is tossing them crumbs, they can usually muster a
smile when someone hands over a signed check.

A few months went by in the new parish. I found other
friendships and learned the idiosyncrasies, sins and strengths
of the people. And then one day toward the end of that first
year, Herman walked into the church office and handed in
his resignation. Actually, he called it retirement; but when a
church treasurer goes out to pasture, you figure there must be
an ulterior motive. After all, who wouldn't enjoy managing
other people's money?

Several months passed before a new sucker could be
recruited, trained and tormented. But by that time, I had
grown used to taking my pay directly out of the offering plate.
A good thing never lasts.

Eventually Herman came back to do some "consulting"
work with the new treasurer. Consultation is a fancy term
that means "I don't know any more about this than you do,
but it sure looks good on a résumé." Herman didn't especially
enjoy this task, for it was one of the many thankless jobs he
had performed over the years. But he did it anyway.

It was at one of these consultation meetings that Herman
first learned about my need for some bookshelves. I don't
recall how the matter came up, but I do remember him telling

me, "I can make you some!" Skeptic that I was, I pointed out that I didn't want just any shelves, I wanted shelving with an air of distinction, shelves that would tell people when they walked into my office, "This guy is a spiritual and intellectual giant."

Herman invited me to his house to look over his operation. What I discovered in back of his home was a tiny shed littered with scraps of wood chips and angled pieces of two-by-fours. Inside he had a table saw, various kinds of drills and lathes, rotors and chisels, and an assortment of hand tools. The place smelled of burnt wood and turpentine.

Herman showed me his lumber collection and asked that I pick out some wood for the shelving. I didn't know the difference between a knotted piece of pine and a fine cut of cherry, so I just told him to use his own judgment. He seemed satisfied enough and told me he would get to work on the shelves right away.

It was clear to me that Herman loved woodworking every bit as much as I liked to read. The time he spent in his workshop was no *work* at all. Rather, it was that one simple pleasure in life that he enjoyed so much he had decided to retire to it. Herman loved to work with wood as much as I loved to work with pages.

During those weeks when Herman was busy with the shelves, I busied myself with unpacking my library. In fact, I added to my collection. Knowing I had shelves coming was like proclaiming an open season on books. I bought and read novels by the dozens, added stacks of biographies, read commentaries and poetry and drama. And all the while, I was writing the same—churning out short stories and essays and novels, most of which have long since been relegated to the recycling bin.

One bright afternoon I was at home reading the *New Yorker* magazine when Herman arrived unexpectedly in his pickup truck and began unloading a set of magnificent handcrafted bookshelves. He had designed the shelves to stack in individual units, each complete with a handhold, stained and varnished to a luster.

We set them up, and when I asked Herman for the bill, he quoted me a ridiculously low sum, telling me that his enjoyment was in the fashioning of the shelves and not in the money he could make from his craft. I gave him some extra money anyway and told him to take his wife out to dinner.

These shelves have come to mean much to me over the years—not only because Herman made them for me with his own hands, but also because one of the greatest pleasures in my life is the simple joy of reading. Every time I remove a book from the shelf I am reminded that much of life's enjoyment is contained in the simple pleasures: reading a novel while reclining in the autumn shade of a willow tree; planting flower bulbs in the rich earth in spring; building a snowman in the backyard; reclining by the fire at first light to read the morning paper; sipping a cup of black coffee; picking apples; gazing up at stars on a clear summer evening as the ocean waves crash upon the shore.

Simple pleasures are the best.

It is the simple pleasure of working with wood that compelled Herman to make something for nothing. I suppose that is why some people whittle, or sew, or garden, or sing. Others like to play instruments, or watch movies, or make a silent space for themselves on the back porch while the dog or cat sleeps soundly in their lap. These are all simple pleasures. But, my, how we struggle to find them.

Take our incessant penchant for work, for example. How many people do you know who never find time to relax? They are always working for something or someone. Even their vacations are "working vacations."

However, when we learn that true happiness is not a commodity we can buy, we begin to see the world in a new light. Little things mean so much more. Our pleasure comes not from receiving the expensive gift, but the one given from the heart. Then we are truly free to enjoy the wonderful world around us.

Before my grandfather's death, he took great enjoyment in sitting by the picture window in the living room of his home. From this vantage point he could watch the birds as they gathered around the feeders he had placed nearby. He enjoyed not only watching the birds, but also trying to identify them.

I think some of his most peaceful moments were spent by the window, looking out upon the birds in their simplicity. Like St. Francis of Assisi, who spoke to the creation around him, my grandfather found tranquillity in the natural order of things.

When I was a child, I was fortunate to enjoy many simple pleasures and to witness the vibrancy of the world around me. Each year my family planted a large garden. I saw firsthand how seeds burst from the soil, grow into plants, and finally produce tasty wonders such as beans, cucumbers, tomatoes and peppers. I raised livestock such as rabbits and goats, and I witnessed the birth of dozens of offspring. I fished for fun, took walks in the woods and often napped in the shade of a favorite oak tree.

Simple pleasures are more than hobbies. They are those

moments that grow out of our human need to be at one with the world, to find solace and comfort in the midst of the craziness around us. These pleasures fulfill our need to be at peace with the world, to be with those we love.

Kite flying is a perfect example. Every spring my wife and I load the kids into our station wagon and drive to a park on the other side of town. We try to pick a warm day when the sun is shining and a breeze is whipping the new buds on the trees. There, standing in a field of freshly mowed grass, we get out the kites, attach the strings and try to see how high we can fly.

I say we are flying because when you fly a kite on a warm spring day, you have the sensation of being up there near the clouds yourself, hovering above the trees, the whole world at your feet. My wife and I seem to love it more than the kids. After a time or two of holding the string, feeling the pull of the wind, the kids grow restless, climb back into the station wagon and start crying for McDonald's (is there any other reason for having a station wagon?). But my wife and I fly on, climbing higher and higher, secretly competing against one another.

Flying a kite is so elemental—just you, the wind and a piece of string. It's as if a person can feel the tug of the forces of nature, way up high. It's like battling the wind. And, for most of us, stringing a kite into the heavens is as close as we can come to flying without ever leaving the ground.

A pleasure such as this takes us on an adventure. For a few moments we are lost in the simplicity of the moment itself, the pure enjoyment of the journey. We can find these pleasures in nature, or we can find them in a crowded room. Mostly, we just find them within ourselves.

Not long ago I participated in a service project in Indianapolis. I had gone to help at a local soup kitchen, arriving early to prepare sandwiches, stir broth and set tables. Everyone worked very hard to ensure that the lunch was tasty and attractive. Finally the guests began arriving. The soup and sandwiches were served. And then it was time to clean up.

However, while most of the volunteers began clearing tables and cleaning bowls, I stayed behind with the guests to talk. I was amazed to see so many smiles on the faces of the homeless. Some of these street people seemed to possess a greater joy for life than did many of the nicely dressed businesspeople who passed them by on the streets. Not all the people were smiling and jovial, of course, but several had discovered their own simple pleasures in the midst of their tragedy.

One lady, I noted, had a plastic bag full of assorted figurines. After lunch she took them out, sat them on the table and began to paint them. She was every bit as proud of her collection of figurines as any person I have known who collects plates, crystal or baseball cards.

Sometimes we forget that everyone needs a hobby. Pastimes are not just for the rich, the retired or the well-to-do. Relaxation and rejuvenation are a necessary component of life. Without putting some energy back into ourselves— sitting for a spell to enjoy a simple pleasure—we tend to burn out quickly. Our minds need to focus on other matters besides worries and cares. Our hands need to be busied by delicate work such as painting or sculpting in lieu of heavy lifting or typing at a keyboard all day. Our bodies need to relax.

Perhaps that is why so many people find pleasure in gardening. There is something meaningful in caring for living

things, watching them grow, bloom and wilt. And the pleasure is not simply in the thing itself, but in the doing.
Gardening is feeling the cool texture of the earth between
one's fingers, pushing grit under the nails, finding the perfect
patch of square soil for the round bulb. Gardening is what
people do when they have run out of patience. Digging in dirt
is a way to relive our childhoods without having other people
stare at us in disbelief. It is culturally acceptable, a way of
overcoming the worries and strains of life.

A lady who lives next door has a green thumb for petunias.
She plants them and pots them all around her house. The
flowers seem to explode with color. As she works, I can sometimes hear her singing or humming. That must mean she is
enjoying her work. Her stress level is down, her heart rate
low, her cholesterol in check. She should live a long time,
enjoying life as she does.

I know she has found meaning in the little things. This
must be true, for she has also experienced her share of
heartache and loss. Being an aging widow, she has known the
grief of losing a husband, has seen her children move out of
the house, has lived alone for a number of years. But she continues to enjoy life because she has found wonder in the little
things, the small daily blessings of existence.

I have seen other people in far worse conditions who have
discovered the simple pleasures. Whenever I visit nursing
care facilities, I take note of the number of residents who
enjoy playing cards, watching television, knitting or working
a puzzle. Some of these residents have Alzheimer's, but they
have latched onto some pastime that is quite important to
them. A few do not even know their next of kin but can still

play the piano flawlessly, sing with perfect pitch or sketch pastoral scenes. The human brain is an astounding organ, and I am amazed at how many older people living in such conditions still have a reason for smiling.

Although we may plan to enjoy certain moments such as reading or painting, it is true that most of life's simple pleasures arrive serendipitously. We don't expect the happy moment when grandchildren climb onto our knees and ask why the sun is shining. We don't expect to find the quiet morning to ourselves after the rest of the family has left the house, giving us time to putter around, eat a leisurely breakfast or smell the fresh scent of the spring air wafting through the window screens. Such moments cannot be arranged; they simply happen.

I'll always remember how much I enjoyed the days immediately following my daughter's birth. Although my wife may have a different recollection of those first two days in the hospital, for me they were some of the most relaxing moments I had experienced in my life. Those days at the hospital were filled with simple pleasures I could never have planned. All the months of waiting were finally over. No one expected anything of me. All the focus was on my wife and new daughter. I felt free to enjoy these days for what they were—an unrepeatable series of events, with family gathered around, celebrating the arrival of a new life.

There was no way I could have bought those moments. I had to sit back and take it all in.

Those evenings, after my wife and daughter had gone to sleep together, I would sit in the rocking chair in the corner and stare at them through the twilight. I could hear my daughter breathing, and I would sit and stare, and wonder about her future. When I felt like it, I would go into the kitchenette across the hall and eat a cup of yogurt or drink a can of pop. I'd walk the empty halls of the maternity ward late at night and do little more than take note of the utter silence of that place. Sometimes I would stop at a window and look out over the city lights, thankful that I had a life to return to and a new daughter to share it with.

But those moments of tranquillity didn't last. They never do.

I'm not sure why we give up on the simple things so easily, or stop anticipating them. Perhaps it is because, as we earn more and spend more, we expect more of our pleasures. We think that the best things of life naturally have to cost more. We begin to reason that if a twenty-five-cent dip of ice cream tastes good, a dollar dip must be four times as good. We know we could walk across the street to appreciate a beautiful garden, but we could also pay thousands of dollars to fly halfway around the world to look at exotic flowers.

Of course nothing is wrong with any of these things, and having enough money to enjoy a rich dish of ice cream and travel the world is a wonderful blessing. But sometimes our logic eludes us. While seeking to find happiness, sometimes we fail to see that it can be found in our own backyards and that it costs nothing.

Life itself is a gift. And the happiness we seek in life can often be found in our attitude and perspective.

Several years ago, when Margaret Thatcher was prime minister of Britain, a terrorist's bomb exploded in the conference room where many of the government meetings were held. Margaret Thatcher survived this blast, but some of her cabinet members were killed.

The following Sunday, Margaret Thatcher went to church as she always did. But that particular Sunday seemed different. As Margaret Thatcher sang the hymns, listened to the message, saw the candles upon the altar and the sunshine streaming through the stained-glass windows, she began to weep. She wept because everything around her had been changed by the loss of her friends. The familiar had now become strange. The goodness and beauty of the world around her seemed almost too much to bear. She knew she would not only miss her friends, but also the wonderful times they had had together.

Often it is in moments of loss that we come to realize the joys of the simple things of life. A bounced check or a failed business venture pales in comparison to the loss of a child. Going through a divorce, losing a job, being forced to move to a new community—all of these changes can cause us to think about those things that are most important to us.

When I sit with families through times of grief and sorrow, I most often hear them talking about the good times they will miss with their loved one. Rarely do families talk about money, estates or business ventures during these times. They talk about love, and opportunities lost, and the simple days they shared together. Most would give anything to find those moments again.

We come to miss the simple things of life when they elude us.

In other instances, we find renewed appreciation for the simple pleasures when we experience hardship or distress. Have you ever been so sick that you would have given anything just to experience a painless moment? Or have you ever been without work to the point where, when you did find a job, you could not understand why you ever grumbled about your previous job?

Perspective matters. Giving in to the sheer joy of life has its own rewards.

I know this was true for Lanna, a friend of mine who underwent a heart transplant a few years ago. For years, Lanna had suffered from an incurable virus that gradually ate away her heart. Her quality of life continued to diminish, but not her optimistic attitude.

Although the prospect of leaving behind her husband and sons was not enticing, she was able to live creatively each day in the hope that a heart donor would one day be found. Finally, unexpectedly, the call came.

Lanna was rushed to the hospital, underwent a quick series of tests to see whether her body was ready for the operation and hours later received confirmation that the heart transplant was a go. Those first few hours after the operation were harrowing indeed. Her family waited anxiously for the doctors to tell them that Lanna had a new lease on life.

Only two days after the operation, I visited with Lanna briefly in the intensive care room. She was hooked up to every conceivable monitor and pump, tubes and wires trellising her body. She was so weak she could hardly smile. I touched her hand.

Then, through gasps of air, she told me what her family was waiting to hear. "I'm going to make it," she said. "But whether I live a day, a month or several years, every day from here on out is gravy. Every day is a day I might not have seen. And I'm going to live every one of them to the fullest."

Lanna did make it. She's still living with that heart. And I know she lives every day to the fullest—gravy, as she called it.

Lanna understood. She could buy the heart transplant, go through the procedure to find a few more days to live, but it was attitude and perspective that gave her the gravy.

Somewhere in life, every one of us longs to discover the simple pleasures that make for happiness and joy. We don't just want to live, we want to be alive. We want tranquillity and peace.

Enjoying a simple pleasure is a moment when we are most fully alive. Whether it be a moment with family or friends, or a time of solitude, these simple pleasures give us serenity. And there are times when we can also give them away.

Not long ago, I happened to see a battered van parked at the side of the road. A sign read: *Roses: $6 a Dozen.* I was standing on the other side of the street waiting for the light to change, but happened to note that several cars had already pulled in behind the van. In every instance, a man got out of the car, walked up to the van and purchased a dozen red roses.

How could I allow a moment like that to pass me by? I knew love when I saw it. And it wasn't even spring.

When the light changed, I walked across the street, shelled out six dollars for the roses and took them home to my wife. It was a simple thing, a small gesture of love, but the pleasure my wife received from the flowers was worth far more than the thing itself. I felt, somehow, that I had added to her day, made our love a bit brighter. Maybe so. Although eventually the roses withered and were thrown into the trash.

But isn't that the case with all simple pleasures? They pass too quickly. They do not last. And we are left with our memories of those special moments.

I know I feel this passing every time I finish reading a great novel. I think: Why did it have to end? Why did the characters have to die? Why couldn't the author have continued for another hundred pages or so?

Perhaps you, too, have experienced such joys. Are you reading this book while lying in a hammock in your backyard, surrounded by bird songs, sipping a glass of lemonade? Or perhaps you are reclining in the easy chair next to the fireplace, a crackling log casting its warmth upon you like a blanket. Or perhaps you are in bed, wrapped in quilts made by your grandmother, the restful sounds of your children easing their way down the hallway in the still silence of evening.

Make an investment in the simple pleasures. Claim them for your own. Look for them and anticipate them in the mundane spaces of your life.

Yes, even give them away. A stuffed animal, a trinket taken idly from a deserted drawer, a hug—what child would not receive these simple gifts with joy? Give your spouse an extra day of vacation or a day of solitude. Give your aging parents a homemade card, an unexpected phone call.

Then, after you have given a few simple pleasures to others, indulge yourself. Find a lawn chair, put on your walking shoes, and take a short trip through the valley and over the hill to that peaceful spot only you know about. Take nothing with you, or take much. Sing as you go, or be silent. Sit for a long time, or stay only a moment.

But sit.

Enjoy.

11

Joyful Laughter

Laugh, and the world laughs with you.

—Ella Wheeler Wilcox

Some years back, when Johnny Carson was host of the *Tonight Show,* he invited an old gentleman to appear as a guest. This fellow (who was nearly one hundred years old) had no claim to fame, no talent or movie credits, but was a plain man full of homespun wisdom. Carson asked him questions, and the fellow shot back commonsense answers. This fellow's down-to-earth, no-nonsense approach to living made the audience howl with delight. This fellow had an opinion about everything from marriage and sex to money and taxes. And he never backed away from any difficult question, but shot straight from the hip. Some of his observations about life were so wonderfully simple that Carson could only smile and nod in agreement.

Mostly, however, this fellow laughed. And he enjoyed making other people laugh. When Carson asked him how he stayed so young, the fellow talked about "being as young as you feel." When Carson asked him whether he had some secret to living that he would like to share with others, the fellow leaned back and told the audience that it was all really quite simple: "Every day when I get up I have two choices. I can choose to be miserable. Or I can choose to be happy. And I choose to be happy. It's as simple as that."

I enjoyed listening to this old fellow because he had many valid points about life and some keen observations about living to share. Mostly, though, I enjoyed his infectious laughter and the way he was able to elicit laughter from others. That is a rare art, and I admire those folks who can make me laugh, especially when I am feeling low.

Laughter—as it has often been described—is the best medicine. *Reader's Digest* even has a regular column, a collection of humorous anecdotes, that takes its title from this maxim. There is truth here. For of all the emotions that can keep us alive and lift us up, humor is the most potent. What would life be without laughter?

Not long ago, at a funeral, I invited family and friends to stand and offer memories or stories about the deceased: a forty-year-old man who had died in a freak accident. I was amazed when the mother stood to give a testimony about her son. Through tears, but with a controlled and passionate determination, she told us how her son was admired by family and friends as a peacemaker. Often, when other people were arguing, her son would step in, make some humorous remark and reduce the two adversaries to laughter. Others admired his sense of humor, and his ability to make people laugh saved many from becoming enemies. In essence, his sense of humor defined him as a human being and served as his greatest gift to others.

I suppose that is why we are fascinated by stand-up comedians, men and women who can get up on a stage and, for a few minutes, make us forget our troubles and allow us to laugh at ourselves. When we learn to take life less seriously, learn to loosen up a little and poke fun at ourselves, life becomes more enjoyable and entertaining. Those who can't laugh, or refuse to laugh, at the strange and sordid affairs of life are missing out on some great fun.

This is one of the reasons, I believe, why the television show M*A*S*H* was such a hit and is still one of the most popular reruns on the air. M*A*S*H* was set against the backdrop of the Korean War, and in terms of dramatic presentation and realism, never shied away from the stark misfortunes and atrocities of war. Every show was written and acted out with these realities in full view. Nearly every episode dealt with some facet of human suffering or misfortune.

But the show also managed to show how humor, even in wartime situations, helped keep people sane and, in fact, was a necessary ingredient to the health and well-being of the doctors, nurses and wounded soldiers who moved through the M*A*S*H* unit. In many episodes this humor came out most effectively in the operating room during moments of intense pressure, when death was imminent and the sufferings of war were most immediate. Without Hawkeye's jokes and shenanigans, the show would have been a flop. But we also have the idea that, without humor, the war itself would have been unbearable.

Laughter helps us to cope with difficult situations and can help to make every day a bit brighter.

I think there is much truth in the notion that we need laughter to secure our sanity and to keep us moving through life with a smile on our face, instead of a scowl. Laughter, in fact, might even be the medicine that makes all the other medicines work better.

At least some doctors think so.

Over the years I have talked to many doctors who seem to be of the opinion that humor and a light-hearted approach to sickness may actually save some of us. More and more, we read about the relationship between attitude and healing, about the spiritual and emotional forces that come to bear upon our physical selves and our health. By and large, I think most doctors and experts would agree that a person who has a good attitude, who can laugh and joke and cut up in the hospital bed before and after a surgical procedure, is far more likely to recover. And if not, at least he or she can go out smiling.

One doctor I know has even gone so far as to say that he prefers not to operate on individuals who are so down that they believe they are not going to make it. According to this physician, folks who are pessimistic about their chances or who can't find even a touch of humor in their lives are far more likely to develop postsurgical complications. He believes that the men and women who can laugh with him before surgery, who can joke and smile with their families, are prime candidates for full recovery.

Laughter can make that kind of a difference in our lives. It might even prove to be the difference between life and death. And there is every reason to believe that laughter is a spiritual force.

There is a chaplain at a large hospital in Indianapolis who makes a habit of not only praying with the patients, but also making them laugh when he enters their room. He wears funny-looking ties as he makes his rounds, or sometimes displays a fake arrow through his head, or carries a hand puppet. He has a full array of jokes for every occasion and is quick with a quip or a quote. His ministry is spiritual, but it comes out in the form of laughter, in the essence of joy.

He believes that being healthy, being spiritual, involves the whole person. In his philosophy, when we are well, we laugh. When we are secure in the love of our family and friends, we smile and enjoy ourselves. Faith teaches this, too.

I've taken this approach in my own ministry. In my office I have several pictures of Jesus—imaginative creations to be sure—which show Jesus in various postures of smiling, delight and hearty laughter. Over the years I've received many comments about these pictures, mostly favorable. Usually people will make comments like "I've never thought about it that way before, but I'm sure Jesus laughed" or "Wow! That puts a whole new spin on the meaning of joy" or "I suppose, if anyone knew how to laugh, it was Jesus."

Every now and again, however, someone will look at those pictures and pucker up like a prune. They just can't seem to accept the image of a smiling or laughing Jesus. They want only a sorrowful Jesus, a sad Jesus, a serious and suffering Jesus. The image of a happy Jesus upsets their stereotype of faith, and they don't know how to deal with it. It's as if their image of God will not allow for laughter; it's as if they have no room for laughter as a spiritual or life-changing force.

It's a strange thing, but often it is the most "religious" folks who have a problem with laughter. They just can't seem to find a connection between God and humor. To them, everything associated with faith should be approached with the utmost seriousness. They walk around looking as if they have been sucking on green persimmons for the better part of a year rather than enjoying the presence and joy of a living God.

Folks can go around scowling if they want to. But I'm keeping my pictures of the laughing Jesus. To me, they are very comforting, and I find in them a representation of God's humor toward the world.

Somehow, I've always had the sneaking suspicion that God is laughing at us anyway. The only thing is, God's laughter comes out in many different forms—and most often through others. All we have to do is listen.

When you and I think about reasons for laughing, bad situations don't come immediately to mind. But how many times have you said to yourself or someone else after a difficulty: "Someday we will look back on this and laugh"?

My wife and I do this all the time. Maybe we'll be in the middle of an argument, or one of us will say something stupid, and then we will start laughing. Most arguments, after all, are based on childish disagreements. If we took the time to think about what we were arguing about from the get-go, we'd have to laugh at our own pettiness most of all. Or, as my grandmother puts it, "Most arguments don't amount to a hill of beans."

Looking back on some of the major arguments in our marriage, my wife and I agree that one of our biggest disagreements occurred the first day of our honeymoon. We were vacationing in Myrtle Beach and were returning to our hotel for the night when I made a driving mistake (I'll go ahead and take the blame for this one even though I know I am right!). I had stopped at an intersection when the light turned yellow, and my wife thought I should have proceeded through the intersection like a bat out of hell (perhaps she was anxious to get back to the room!).

One word led to another, an argument ensued and before we knew it, we were engaged in a mortal combat concerning our differing driving philosophies. She was pointing and screaming at me, and I was screaming at her. At one point I slapped my wife on the knee—harder than I intended to, much too forceful for her taste—and immediately I had visions of sleeping in the hotel lobby near the vending machines.

Somehow, before we returned to the hotel, I managed to smooth-talk my way into her heart again, and she actually let me in the room. Later (much later!), we were able to laugh about this argument. In fact, it is one of the few things we actually remember about our honeymoon, and it has served us well over the years, especially since we visited the lawyer and signed our agreement never to ride together in the same car.

Laughter can crop up anywhere—at the supermarket, at the office, even at the dinner table.

An older friend of mine talks about the morning he and his wife sat down to eat breakfast. She was at the stove cooking up a mess of bacon and eggs. When they sat down together to eat, my friend casually reached over, took the salt and pepper shakers, and doctored up his eggs. Immediately his wife exploded, "Don't do that! I salted and peppered those eggs while they were frying in the pan!"

"Why on earth would you do that?" my friend shot back. "Everyone knows you salt and pepper food at the table."

"No," his wife insisted, "you salt and pepper food while it's cooking."

"At the table!"

"While it's cooking!"

"At the table!"

"While it's cooking!"

They went back and forth like this for some time before one of them eventually broke down and started laughing. Here they were, two grown people, arguing about salt and pepper.

Such arguments may seem paltry, but I've known couples who have ended their marriages over less satisfying arguments than that. Sometimes laughter is the only thing that saves two people from killing each other.

Before a couple has their first argument about how to squeeze the toothpaste tube, or how to balance the checkbook, or how to make a bed, they should learn to laugh together. That's my theory. Without laughter, even the little things can get under the skin, infect a relationship and destroy it. Possessing the ability to find humor in the mundane affairs of living together is a life-saving quality.

Humor can even lighten the air during moments of intense stress. A story told years ago by a retired bishop when I was in seminary related such a case.

It seems this bishop and three of his episcopal pals were on a transatlantic flight to Europe back in the 1950s. They were seated near the rear of the plane—an old four-engine prop job—when a woman seated just a few rows ahead of them let out a blood-curdling scream. A stewardess came running down the aisle, and the woman proceeded to gesture toward the window where, on the wing, one of the four propellers had ground to a halt.

"Look out there," the frightened woman told the stewardess. "That propeller is not moving! Something's wrong. We're going to crash!"

The stewardess tried to calm the passenger, but the woman insisted the plane was going to crash. "We're going down! Look—that propeller is not moving!"

The stewardess calmly explained why there was no danger. "This plane has four engines. If we have to, we can fly with only one engine. So you see, there's nothing to be frightened about."

For a moment it appeared that the woman accepted the explanation and would remain calm, but each time the stewardess passed, the woman pointed out the window toward the stalled propeller. "We've got to do something," she insisted. "Turn back. Set this thing down. We're in trouble."

Suddenly the stewardess turned around and noticed the four clergymen sitting at the rear of the plane. She walked back to the bishop and his cohorts. "Are you pastors?" she asked.

"We're bishops," came the reply, "on our way to a big episcopal summit in Europe."

"Oh," the stewardess sighed. "Thank God. Now I can put that woman's mind at ease once and for all."

With that word, the bishops watched as the stewardess approached the woman. The stewardess tapped her on the shoulder and said, "Ma'am, did you know that on board this plane there are four bishops? Now, don't you think that with four bishops on board, surely God will watch over us? I mean, there's no way we are going to crash with four bishops on this plane."

The woman turned in her seat, glanced back at the four smiling bishops. She turned to the other side and stared out the window at the immobile propeller. Then she looked up at the stewardess and said, "Well, if it's all the same to you, I'd rather have four good engines than four bishops any day."

Now think for a moment about the question "What makes you laugh?" No doubt you would be able to produce a nice list. You might even have difficulty getting to the end of it.

Like most things in life, when we sit down and produce a mental list of blessings and highlights, we come to realize very quickly how fortunate we are and how truly good life has been. As we go about our days, working and hoping and striving for the future, we can miss the here-and-now moments and the one-of-a-kind events that will live forever in our memory. It doesn't take much to set us on edge and keep us from enjoying the little things. That's where laughter comes in. And that's why we need it.

I write a column called "Malebag" for a bridal magazine. Each issue affords me the opportunity to explore another dimension of marriage from a male perspective—hence the title of the column.

A few issues back I wrote about the humorous habits of the average American male. My research for this column consisted of conversations with friends, a few phone calls and a bit of reading in psychology journals. But all things pointed to the same conclusion: Men find humor in certain television shows and situations, and the male laugh-o-meter is generally tuned differently than the female.

Consider, for example, the type of humor of the Three Stooges. Most men are reduced to tears by the crazy antics and slapstick humor of these idiots. Most women, on the other hand, consider these antics to be childish and a complete waste of time. Women generally don't laugh at physical humor.

While writing this column, I also found that, according to several studies of male and female habits, men tend to touch other men far more often than women touch other women. This is especially true when men laugh and joke with one another. Men will generally slap each other on the back or the thigh following the punch line of a joke. They will lean toward each other and sometimes offer a fake punch to the ribs. Women, on the other hand, more frequently laugh and joke with one another at a distance. Male humor tends to lean toward the visual and the physical. Women's humor tends to lean toward the auditory and the cerebral.

These, of course, are broad generalizations, but I think they hold true in the marketplace of laughter. The differences between the sexes are often the source of some of our richest humor.

Comic strips, especially, play on the male/female differences. Strips like *Blondie*, *Andy Capp*, *Hagar the Horrible* and *The Born Loser* all poke fun at male/female relationships and stereotypes. In the comic strip *Blondie*, Dagwood is often portrayed as a "typical" man, a fellow with little feeling for romance or communication. Blondie, on the other hand, always seems to have the perfect answer for Dagwood and the family. Likewise, Andy Capp would rather spend time with his friends, and his wife always has to bail him out of trouble. Even Hagar the Horrible—a real man's man—is no match for his wife when it comes to wit or a test of wills. The Born Loser and his wife are often portrayed as a typical married couple who can't seem to win at anything. A great many of these comic strips address aspects of marriage and love that may remind us of ourselves and help us to laugh at our situations.

A great many jokes also hit upon aspects of marriage that often remind us of ourselves. Such is the case of the older gentleman who was being examined by his doctor. When the doctor finished he said, "How old did you say you were, sir?"

"Eighty-eight," came the reply.

"Eighty-eight! Sir, you have the body of a sixty-year-old. What's your secret?"

The fellow explained: "Well, when my wife and I got married, we agreed that we would settle every argument in the following manner: When she got mad, she would go to the kitchen to calm down. When I got mad, I would keep my mouth shut and go outside until I calmed down."

The doctor looked puzzled. "I don't understand," he said. "How has that helped you to stay so fit?"

"Well," the fellow explained, "let's just say that I've lived an outdoor life."

Often, when I'm reading the newspaper, I guffaw at the plights of human beings in all of their resplendent glory. Some of the true-life accounts of human foibles and mistakes are the best humor we can find. Or, as the old saying goes, truth is stranger than fiction. We don't have to look past our newspapers to find a reason to laugh.

In other news, a Belgian thief was once caught in the act of burglarizing a house. As he fled the scene, he exited out a back door, ran past policemen and guards, scaled a nine-foot wall topped with barbed wire, dropped to the ground, and found himself inside the city prison.

Every day it seems, if we read the newspaper or listen to the news with an ear for humor, we can find something to laugh about. Someone, somewhere, is making a fool of himself. Somebody else is giving us a reason to laugh at the strange twists and turns of life.

Folks who want to hear or see only doom and gloom are missing out on quite a funny ride. They are also missing an opportunity to be happy.

I've got a friend, Charlie, who bears a striking resemblance to Colonel Sanders—the famous fried-chicken king. Charlie is nearing one hundred years of age, and yet he is full of the vim and vigor of life. He loves to laugh, and he is constantly on the lookout for tidbits of humor and laughable quotes. He collects these in a notebook every month and sends out a newsletter to friends and family. I'm on his mailing list.

Last month he sent me a collection of quotes that he had gleaned from various sources. I pass a few of them along to you.

Waking up in the morning is a matter of mind over mattress.

You know you've reached middle age when your weight training consists of standing up.

Going to the beach is like cleaning the attic—you never know what you're going to find in trunks.

Stockroom clerk: someone who's shelf-employed.

By the time you're rich enough to sleep late, you're so old you wake up early every morning.

Pop singer: someone who sings through his nose by ear.

Once you and I have an idea that we want to live well, we might as well learn to laugh. Life's too short to make it any other way.

Just ask my friend Charlie.

12

Natural Wonders

This is my letter to the world,
That never wrote to me,—
The simple news that Nature told,
With simple majesty.

—Emily Dickinson

Not long ago, on a beautiful autumn day, I felt the irre-
sistible tug of nature and decided to leave behind the trappings of my office for a walk in the woods. That afternoon I
slipped on a pair of ragged tennis shoes—the ones I normally
wear when I mow the lawn—and set out on an excursion to
who knows where. On this particular journey, the autumn
was so dry that the leaves were vibrant with color. The soft
maples had traded in their green leaves for a burst of yellow.
The oaks were a flame of wild fire and burnt orange. The crab
apple and sycamore had blossomed into violet and gold.

I walked an uncertain path, meandering over swells and beyond the shallow ravines where the creeks had carved their summer courses. Near the creek beds I noted animal prints—deer and raccoon, bird and coyote. When the wind shifted, the leaves rustled overhead and I could smell the rich decay of the earth beneath my feet. Certain elements of nature were dying. Others were clinging to life. Most were being transformed, going into hibernation, preparing to bloom again in the spring. Death would come. But there would be a rebirth.

As I walked on, I came to a clearing where several walnut trees had been harvested the preceding summer. Here, in piles of limbs amid the brush, the remaining vestiges of these giants lay to rot in the winter snows—another death giving way to new life.

I sat on one of the stumps to rest and felt a calm sweep over me, a feeling of tranquillity that cannot be named. Rising like spires around me, the new growth of walnut trees, of maples and oaks, sang a chorus in the breeze as their colors danced overhead. One phase of nature was passing away, another was approaching and I felt as if I were sitting at the convergence of the two. I was witnessing an end and a beginning at one and the same time.

Through a clearing in the trees I saw evidence of another harvest—a cornfield shaved to a stubble of stalks. Beyond that, shimmering in the afternoon sun, I saw the steel grain bins of the farm, the harvest come home, the grain ready to be transported and refined into meal.

At peace on the stump, I hearkened back to another episode in my life when I had witnessed something of a coldness in the human spirit, a kind of antithesis of nature and the beauty of creation. I had gone to visit an elderly widow who was confined to her home (though I found out right away that she was neither elderly nor confined and that the place where she lived had none of the warmth of a home). This woman made such an impression on me that, to this day, whenever I think of her, a cold chill runs down my spine.

When I entered her home, I discovered immediately why many folks assumed she was a shut-in and could not get out. All her blinds were pulled tightly over the windows. No sunlight ever fell upon her artificial plants. Her car was shut up securely in the garage behind the house.

From the outset it was clear that this woman did not particularly appreciate my visit. I had disturbed her space, and she related to me as if I were an alien from another planet. I had come from the "outside"—a world that seemed to frighten her—and disturbed the delicate cocoon she had created for herself.

When I greeted her, I mentioned that it was a beautiful day—plenty of sunshine, crisp air, perfect temperature, summer flowers in full bloom. She was quick to point out that the extended forecast was calling for rain in a day or two and that it was going to be nasty and cold before we knew it. I changed the subject, told her a few things that were taking place in the parish, mentioned the names of a few people she might know. Again her response was negative.

In the course of our conversation, this woman inevitably returned to a common theme: The world was a nasty, ugly place filled with nasty, ugly people. "There's so much bad stuff out there," she kept saying. "Murder and rape and madness. People killing each other on the street for a thin dime."

"Yes," I told her, "there are many problems. But isn't it a wonderful life? Didn't God give us a beautiful world?"

She looked at me as if I had lost my mind.

Then it struck me! Looking around her living room, I noted that the television in the corner had been running full blast since I had entered. A talk show host was interviewing women who had, supposedly, found true love in the arms of the men who had murdered their boyfriends. Beside her recliner was a two-foot-high stack of tabloid magazines. A solitary light bulb hung from the ceiling. There was no color, nothing to give life or vibrancy to the room. All her perceptions of the world around her came not from her experience of reality, but from a television tube, a tabloid magazine or a bad dream.

I felt a deep sense of pity for her. She saw no beauty, no wonder, no delight in the world.

Sitting there in her living room, many questions crossed my mind: Have you ever looked out your window and watched the children playing at the school across the street? Have you ever planted a flower and nourished it until a first frost? Have you ever eaten a peach and felt the juices running down your chin? Have you ever seen a sunset? Have you ever walked the woods in spring and felt the wind upon your face and the sun upon your back? Have you ever rolled in fresh snow? Have you ever sat on the beach at sunrise and gazed upon the vastness of the world? Have you ever stretched out in the evening grass and observed the infinite stars on a clear summer night? Have you ever listened to a bird's song or watched an eagle soaring above a mountain peak? Have you ever smelled the sweet scent of freshly mowed hay? Have you ever touched the heart of the milkweed? Have you ever sat in your living room near a crackling fire, or read a good book, or had warm and pleasant conversations with friends?

More than a hundred years ago, Walt Whitman celebrated the joy of life and the wonders of nature in his immortal collection of poems, *Leaves of Grass*. This masterpiece revolutionized American literature and suggested that life is most fully appreciated when we live in harmony with the created order. Like many of the psalms of the Bible, *Leaves of Grass* gave testimony to the boundless universe and sang of the sheer delight and beauty of the world.

When Whitman wrote:

> *Prais'd be the fathomless universe*
> *For life and joy, and for objects and knowledge curious,*
> *And for love, sweet love—But praise! praise! praise!*
> —"When Lilacs Last in the Door-yard Bloom'd"

he was celebrating the wonders of nature and our oneness with the world. Even in the midst of a terrible civil war and the mounting loss of human life, Whitman was able to sing the eternal joy of witnessing nature's beauty and life-giving balm.

Rather than turning inward in times of distress and weariness, Whitman sang of turning outward to the power of nature. Even though life has its share of turmoil and difficulties, sometimes cruelties and atrocities, there is still the serene, small voice of wonder and delight that comes to us in the beauty of a sunset, the turning of the autumn leaves, the fragrance of a flower. Whitman understood this when he wrote:

> *Roaming in thought over the Universe,*
> *I saw the little that is Good steadily*
> *hastening toward immortality,*

And the vast that is Evil I saw hastening
to merge itself and become lost and dead.

—"Roaming in Thought After Reading Hegel"

I wonder where you and I would be if not for the energy and joy we gain, even unknowingly, from the life-giving sustenance of the earth? At every moment, you and I consume the life that comes to us through these wonders of nature. The oxygen we breathe comes from trees and vegetation. The water that makes life possible comes from the rivers and oceans, which, in turn, come from the heavens. Our bodies are sustained and nourished through the consumption of other living things—animals and plants, berries and buds and fruits and vegetables. Without this life around us, we would soon cease to exist as well.

Understanding our dependency upon the wonders of nature should serve to make us more wise in our consumption and more celebrative of the loveliness of the earth and all living things. As the traditional Jewish table blessing suggests, we are utterly dependent upon our Maker, who provides our sustenance through the natural world: "Blessed are you, O Lord, who brings forth bread from the earth."

None of us has to look far to find delight and awe in the grandness of the universe. Even if we live in the city, surrounded by honking cars and concrete, we can observe the tiniest of miracles: a weed growing from a crack in the sidewalk; the intricacies of a leaf; the shapes and faces of clouds floating overhead. Nature is all around us. There is no way we can flee from the pervasive presence of creation.

So sings the psalmist:

The heavens are telling the glory of God;
and the firmament proclaims his handiwork.
Day to day pours forth speech,
and night to night declares knowledge.
There is no speech, nor are there words;
their voice is not heard;
yet their voice goes out through all the earth,
and their words to the end of the world.

—Ps. 19:1–4 NRSV

The first time I began to sense my connectedness with the natural world was when I was a self-absorbed teenager. Behind our house were two farm ponds where, from spring to autumn, I often wandered to fish or to sit on the bank of a pond to read a book. Here I began to note the sharp outlines of the trees, their distinctive shapes, and grew to know the contour of the land by heart. These frequent forays into the woods became quite meaningful to me and, through the years, I have longed to recover much of the tranquillity of those days.

Living close to nature, I noted the interconnectedness of all things and learned to appreciate the work of tending a garden, raising livestock and putting seed back into the earth for the next year. When an animal died, we buried it in the ground as fertilizer for the crops. Instead of throwing away unproductive bean plants or withered vines, we fed them to the animals. Much of the refuse and waste was recycled, utilized in other ways. I learned to appreciate clean water and trees and mulched leaves. Very little was wasted.

I suppose that many of the people who frequent city parks or visit the more scenic national forests are seeking to find this same oneness with the natural order. There is something within the human spirit that causes us to reach out for the sunshine and the sea, to climb into our cars and drive to the nearest green spot, or to visit a natural history museum or a zoo and stroll amid the wildlife. Maybe there is something of the wild animal remaining in us that causes this stirring, this longing for the wide-open spaces and the mountain slope. Or perhaps it is something of heaven itself, a hope that all things might live once more in the harmony of Eden.

Regardless, we experience these sudden lapses, these urges to return to something basic, instinctual. We want the sand and the sea and the sun, and we want to know that there is yet something in this world that we have not seen, that we have not experienced. That is why, I suppose, people climb mountains, or dive into the depths of the sea, or disappear into jungles in search of some undiscovered species. We are not alone in the world, and we are blessed for it. We have not yet discovered all of the secrets of the universe, nor even the secrets contained upon the earth, and we are startled by what we do not know through the depth of our knowing.

Truly, the wonders of nature amaze us. And the earth is filled with many strange and marvelous creatures.

Consider the African reed frog. Found in East Africa, this tiny frog has baffled scientists for decades. Years ago, when the frog was being studied by researchers, scientists found that this creature could remain exposed to the intense African sun for up to one hundred days and never burn. While studying this frog's amazing sun-blocking powers, however, the researchers made an even more amazing discovery: the female frogs, when outnumbered by males by more than three to one, could switch sexes if needed to reproduce the species. This process of changing from female to male takes several months, and is never reversed.

Another frog, found predominantly in South America, is one of the few species on earth who have babies that are larger than the adults. When the tadpoles are hatched, they grow to be seven to ten inches in length and then, as they mature into frogs, actually shrink in size.

It seems that every day we can read about some new discovery in the realm of the animal kingdom. In the past decade, new toxins and secretions have been discovered among rain forest insects and amphibians that some believe may help combat diseases. Other biologists continue to learn about the intricate balance that exists between indigenous animals and the natural environment. One discovery leads to another, and another.

When we think about the wonders yet to be found in nature, and the possibility of life-giving discoveries, we cannot help but feel compelled to do all we can for the preservation of species. Disrupting the natural balance will certainly have irreversible results. Every creature has something to offer to the natural order and to the betterment of humanity.

However, as if the wonders of earth were not enough to humble us, consider also the vastness of the universe and the mounting discoveries being made in space. When the Hubble telescope began sending back pictures from its vantage point 370 miles above the earth, scientists were amazed at how deep this telescope could peer into the universe. Considering that the speed of light is some 186,000 miles per second, and that it takes this long for light to travel from any given point to the next, the Hubble telescope is actually looking back into time,

witnessing the explosion of stars and nebulae, and the colli-
sion of galaxies, that took place some 11 billion years ago.

With the help of the Hubble telescope, scientists have
learned that the universe is vaster and deeper than imagined.
When scientists aimed Hubble's aperture at one of the emp-
tiest parts of the sky, focusing on a portion of space about the
size of a grain of sand, they were amazed to find that even the
darkest regions of space are filled with billions of stars and
untold number of galaxies.

Closer to home, the Hubble telescope took the first high-
resolution image of the planet Pluto, and snapped photos of
Mars and Jupiter that were so clear that scientists could see
cloud formations on Mars and the shadows of moons as they
orbited the giant planet, Jupiter. Even the rings of Saturn
offered new discoveries.

Gazing into the heavens at night, most of us give little
consideration to the vastness of the universe. We may enjoy
the serenity of the stars or feel a slight sense of awe, but the
intricacies of the heavens elude us. When we hear talk of pro-
tons and neutrons, of quarks and black holes and light years,
we can scarcely grasp these concepts. More and more there is
a growing gap between what scientists are discovering and
what is understood by the average person.

I'm not sure how we will bridge this gap of knowledge, but
there is no doubt that, in many respects, science will continue to dictate our future. After all, human beings have
slowly been making strides toward the heavens and, in the
last thirty years, have launched more than seventy spacecraft
to study celestial bodies. These spacecrafts have landed on
the Moon, on Venus and on Mars.

Currently there is talk of having a manned expedition to the red planet. But the culmination of that reality may be a decade or two down the road. In 1997, NASA launched a spacecraft called *Cassini*, which will explore the Saturn system. This probe will approach Saturn's moon, Titan, in the year 2004 and will deploy a smaller craft to explore the surface of this moon. The distance this ship will travel in its seven-year journey staggers the mind.

Other celestial bodies close to earth have also yielded new secrets in the past decade.

We have discovered that Venus has a surface temperature of nearly nine hundred degrees Fahrenheit and that Mars, some 4 billion years ago, had an Earth-like climate. Scientists have also discovered that one of Saturn's moons, Titan, is raining organic molecules onto the planet's surface and that comets might contain a sizable portion of organic matter inside their cores.

Such discoveries make the wonders of nature all the more awesome and grand. Looking at the stars, or seeing photographs of Earth from the space shuttle or from the Russian space station, *Mir*, help us realize that the world is shared by all. Every person depends upon the blessings of the earth for food, water and air. Our ability to survive apart from the earth's grip is limited, at best.

Long before the space age, people recognized the importance of the natural world. Maybe even more so than we do today.

Consider, for example, Henry David Thoreau. In 1845, he began an experiment in simplistic living, taking up residence in a hut he had constructed near the shore of Walden Pond in Concord, Massachusetts. For two years he lived off the land, made notes of his observations about nature and the woodland life that filled the area around the pond. He planted beans. He fished. He also read books, kept copious journals regarding the joys of solitude and of being one with nature, and made friends with the animals and birds. He listened, watched, and attempted to read something of value and virtue into the smallest of nature's wonders and the most intricate of the earth's delights.

Although his book, *Walden*, did not meet with any critical or financial success in his lifetime, Henry David Thoreau gave the world a peek at the happiness one can derive from living close to the earth and enjoying the fruits of nature. His work demonstrates that, even before the beginning of the twentieth century, tranquillity and a closeness to the natural world were rare commodities in daily experience—at least in New England. They are even rarer today.

In *Walden*, Thoreau writes beautifully of the innocence and joy we long to find in the wonders of nature:

> *Every morning was a cheerful invitation to make my life of equal simplicity, and I may say innocence, with Nature herself. I have been as sincere a worshipper of Aurora as the Greeks. I got up early and bathed in the pond; that was a religious exercise, and one of the best things which I did. They say that characters were engraven on the bathing tub of King Tching-thang to this effect: "Renew thyself completely each day; do it again, and again, and forever again."*

I wonder how most of us would fare in such an adventure of simplistic living? I wonder how I would make out among the chipmunks and the squirrels, having to forage for my own food and draw my own water? I am afraid I have grown too dependent upon the supermarket and the electric company to make out well in such an experiment.

The last time I went into the woods it was to participate in something we call "camping"—which is a modern-day invention of city folks who wish to do penance for eating out of boxes, sleeping on water beds and enjoying frozen foods. The first night out it rained heavily and the water seeped through the tent and formed a puddle near my head. I dreamed I was swimming laps and, when I awoke in the morning, I found I had a frog in my throat (you can take that any way you want). I shivered the entire day as I yearned for the warmth of the television set, the microwave oven and the computer screen. By the time the camping excursion was over, I had repented of living a life of luxury and had lost three pounds, but was no closer to nature than when I first set out to start a fire by rubbing two sticks together.

No, I think for most of us, appreciating the wonders of nature will have to take a different form. We may have to look a bit more deeply into ourselves instead of looking for something beyond. And we may have to learn to appreciate the beauty of nature through the daily sleight of hand we experience in the sparrow and the bumble bee, the turning of leaves and the clean aroma following the rain. The wonders of nature are all around us, and they are ours to be enjoyed. All we have to do is look and listen.

What about you? Do you need a little more nature in your life? A little more of the sun and the moon and the stars?

Try turning off the television some evening. Climb into your car and take a drive into the country. Park near a grassy field.

Unroll a blanket, sit for a spell under the stars and just listen.

You'll be amazed at all the things you've been missing— and all the things you hear.

And what you don't.

PART FIVE

The End of
the Day

13

Good Health

Health is better than wealth.

—traditional proverb

Ⓗow many times have you said it or heard someone else say it? *If you have good health, you have everything;* or *You can have all the money in the world, but you can't buy good health.*

More than any of life's blessings, good health enables us to enjoy all the other blessings in their fullness. We know that money cannot buy health, any more than money can buy love or happiness or peace of mind. Oh, we can pay for the best care that money can buy, hook our bodies up to the latest technological gizmos and gadgets, but good health, as we all know, involves so much more than a beating heart and a functioning brain. When we say we are in good health, we are also talking about an attitude and a state of mind as well as bodily well-being.

Good health comes in many different forms, but it always involves a whole person.

When I was in college, I had a friend named Jack who was confined to a wheelchair. Jack had been paralyzed from the waist down in a car accident. In spite of this condition, however, Jack displayed a zest and eagerness and love for life that far surpassed that of his peers. Although Jack could not walk (and I'm certain he had days when he felt anger or loss because of his condition), he refused to see himself as anything other than a whole person. Though his legs didn't work, he had a healthy mind, heart and spirit. He taught me much about the meaning of health.

Consider also the many people who have perfectly healthy bodies, yet lack the necessary components of a healthy mind and attitude. They have the physical capacity to run and jump and do handstands, and yet lack peace of mind. Is this the definition of good health?

More and more we are learning that there is a correlation between the body and the mind, between the physical self and the spiritual/emotional self. In the past decade, a number of books have been written by doctors and health experts about this symbiosis of body and soul. Good health is a matter of being a whole person—finding the balance of the physical, the emotional and the spiritual that leads to a healthy life and to true happiness.

No, money can't buy health any more than it can buy love. And sometimes wealth produces some of the most unhealthy individuals.

Take Diamond Jim Brady, for instance. Here was a famous American who made a fortune during the golden age of the locomotive. Diamond Jim was a household name at the turn of the century, a wealthy man who lived the fast life and strutted his opulence during the Gay Nineties. Brady would travel the country for months at a time, sleeping in the finest hotels, throwing wild parties among New York's elite. He would buy out entire sections of a theater for his friends during a first-night showing on Broadway, and he could be found in gambling houses well into the wee hours of the morning, throwing away money by the bundles to feed his habit.

Diamond Jim got his nickname, of course, from his extensive jewelry collection. It is said that his diamond collection alone totaled more than twenty thousand diamonds, and he had well over six thousand other gems, including twenty-one complete sets of diamond-studded cuff links, rings, scarf pins and shirt studs.

Brady, however, for all of his brashness and glitter, was considered a very unhealthy man by the people who knew him best. His breakfast diet frequently consisted of the following: fried eggs, steaks and chops, mounds of pancakes and potatoes, grits, corn bread, and milk. For lunch he often ate steak and lobster, oysters and clams, and cuts of pie finished off with a box of chocolates. And I won't mention his dinner fare.

By the time Brady was fifty-five years old, he showed signs of physical burnout. In 1912, he was admitted to Johns Hopkins, where it was discovered that he was suffering from gallstones. Doctors there had to build a special operating table and bed to support Brady's heft. When they began the operation, they found that Diamond Jim's stomach was six times normal size and was covered by such a thick layer of fat that they could not operate successfully. Miraculously, Brady recovered—this time.

Immediately after his recovery, Diamond Jim plunged himself headlong into his old lifestyle, paying women to dance with him and tossing money about as if the well would never run dry. He bought a thousand-dollar-a-week apartment overlooking the Atlantic City boardwalk. Within a few weeks, diabetes, bad kidneys and heart pain caught up with him. His well was running dry—and fast.

During the last weeks of his life, all he could do was sit in his apartment and stare at the walls. Brady was found dead in his apartment by his valet on the morning of April 13, 1917; the cause was a massive heart attack.

Although Diamond Jim's lifestyle may indeed appeal to many people, even Brady himself understood that his bad habits and bodily neglect would be his undoing. He was frequently overheard to say that good health was not what it was cracked up to be and that he preferred to die young, so long as he could go eating and drinking and doing the things he enjoyed.

Of course, some people share Brady's philosophy of life—live hard and fast, and burn out while you're young. Most people who long for happiness, however, know they will never find it in this manner. Good health *is* what it's cracked up to be. We want to enjoy the sunshine and the fresh air and the warmth of good friendships. Freedom from physical pain means a great deal when we are trying to live for others. Life itself is the greatest gift of all, and there is so much to see and so little time—even if we live to be a hundred years old.

In my office, I have a special painting. It was given to me years ago by a woman who enjoyed abundant happiness, although she lived with great physical pain. Margaret spent the better part of each day in bed, hooked to a portable oxygen machine. Her breathing came in snatches. But in between these bouts of shortness of breath, Margaret painted with joy.

One would have thought that the pain would have driven the desire from her body, but Margaret loved to create. She lived to paint for others. Unlike her circumstances, her paintings were cheerful, uplifting and bright. Most of her pictures featured blue skies and sunshine.

Her gift to me was a painting of a small house nestled among a thicket of trees. Overhead a billowy white cloud floats across a clear, azure sky. On the back of the painting, she wrote: "The sun is always shining . . . if you look for it."

Whenever Margaret and I talked, she liked to remind me that good health was something to be treasured. "Do all that you can while you're young," she'd say. "It's tough growing old!"

Indeed, I find that as I get older, I appreciate good health all the more.

There are so many things that could happen to us in life. Because of this, the world seems particularly wonderful when we have the good fortune to stroll in its beauty and to mark the days by feeling the sunshine upon our faces. A person who is older but still able to drive a car and have a measure of independence is doubly blessed.

Not long ago, I happened to find a seat next to several older men who were sitting on a park bench, blatantly enjoying a beautiful autumn day. The World Series was just under way, and they were talking baseball and strategy and numbers. Their voices were filled with energy and opinion as they discussed and argued their respective cases. I pretended to read a book, but I was spellbound by their conversation and their passion.

Finally, after the required swaggering and bragging was over, one of the fellows rose to his feet, leaned his weight against his cane, and said, "Beautiful day, my friends. Just beautiful."

I counted that a picture of health and one that I am not likely to forget soon. Sometimes, when we truly want to enjoy the pleasures of health, we have to go looking for an opportunity.

More and more, people are discovering the benefits of staying in shape. Because we have entered an era when most of our jobs require little or no physical exertion, our bodies can waste away behind a desk or in front of the television. Our bodies need to *do* something to stay healthy. And the more, the better. Exercise is now big business, and people are often willing to pay large prices to stay in shape.

But it doesn't have to be so difficult. I've exercised religiously for years, and I've discovered that the key is finding an activity that I enjoy, and then having a friendly competition with myself in order to promote constant improvement week after week. If I walk around the block, I like to see how fast I can complete the circuit. If I lift weights, I like to keep track of how much and how many times I am able to lift a particular weight. If I play basketball, I like to count the number of minutes I am able to run without getting tired. You don't have to invest large sums of money (or any money for that matter) to keep the body in condition.

When my wife and I moved to our current home, we were amazed at the number of families we saw walking around the neighborhood each evening. We saw younger couples in jogging outfits, retired couples in slacks and T-shirts. Some families pushed strollers along or walked their dogs. Others rode bicycles or walked with ankle weights.

My wife and I decided that we couldn't allow the neighbors to have all the fun, so we started walking, too. Usually we took the kids along so the neighbors would see that we were good parents and make favorable comments about us. This worked for the most part, except for those times when my son wandered off the road and picked flowers out of someone's yard.

Eventually my wife came to the upscale conclusion that we all needed bicycles. First we purchased a new bike for my daughter and taught her how to ride. And then we found a little bike with training wheels for my four-year-old son. Finally my wife found a bike that she liked in a mail-order catalog. She rode around the neighborhood about three times with the kids before I got the slick idea that I would enjoy riding her bicycle, too. After all, if my wife gets something nice, I deserve the same consideration. So I took one ride around the block with my son. When we returned home, I found that my weight had warped the back wheel. No more bicycling for me. I'll stick to walking and picking flowers from the neighbor's yard.

I suppose you could follow my lead, or you could find other ways to enjoy your good health. Take hikes in the countryside. Walk the mall every morning. Work outside moving dirt in the garden. Rake leaves. Shovel snow. Walk a treadmill. Jog. Lift. Shoot baskets. Swim. The list could go on and on.

I've even seen older men and women who have taken up in-line skating. I see them at the park, skating down the sidewalk covered with knee pads, elbow pads and hard-shell helmets. More power to them.

Staying in shape was never meant to be tedious. Enjoying our bodies should be fun. The more we put into ourselves and our good health, the more we will get out of ourselves later. After all, eventually we will all fall prey to the ravages of old age, if not before. We might as well enjoy every day to the fullest.

Having worked as a chaplain in a hospital, and because I have held the hand of many a sick person, I believe that most people don't fully comprehend the wonder of good health until they fall prey to an illness. I've heard people in hospital beds recovering from surgeries groan, "My God, I'd give anything to be relieved of this pain," as if in prayer. Others have spoken of good health as a longing for a utopian paradise, far beyond their reach, as if to say, "I know I'll never be the same again." Still others seem to resign themselves to the inevitable: "I'm not going to get well, but at least I can see my grandchildren one last time."

As I've made my way through hospital corridors and funeral home hallways over the years, I've often asked myself: *Why is there so much sickness, and why do we treat our bodies so badly?* I haven't arrived at too many answers, but some folks seem to have strong opinions on the subject.

During my chaplaincy at a large hospital in North Carolina, I shared an evening shift with a young doctor who became a good friend and confidant. He and I worked on a floor of the hospital where many patients came to die. Some of the nurses referred to this floor as "the last stop before the mortuary." Sometimes, as the evening wore on and the patients began to fall asleep, the doctor and I would go to the lounge and talk.

"You ever wonder why there are so many sick people?" I once asked.

"Every day," he answered. "But I find it even more amazing to wonder why more of us are *not* sick." Here he would point to study after study that revealed that most of us live very unhealthy lives. Many drink too much. Many are overweight. Others neglect regular exercise and good foods. Some of us are inclined toward unhealthy habits. Few of us sleep well. Many work too hard and play too little. Most of us do not have regular checkups.

By the time the doctor finished, my mind was reeling. I often wondered why I was not sick, given the multitude of diseases and bad habits that were loosed upon the world. I felt sick just listening to the possibilities.

But, compared to the people who were dying in that hospital ward, I was a specimen of robust health. It was later, months after I had decided that hospital chaplaincy was not my forte, that I learned the unspoken truth about many of the people who were dying on that floor.

They had AIDS.

This was in the early 1980s, when AIDS was just beginning to come to the forefront of national attention, and there were few people in the health professions who would even say the acronym. I was amazed that, in all the time I spent on that hospital floor, I never once heard AIDS mentioned aloud. Likewise, looking back on my experience, only one nurse ever cautioned me to be wary of needle pricks or about touching a patient's blood emission without gloves. Maybe it was for the best because I did not worry about these things and, consequently, never stopped reaching out.

Being with those patients—holding their hands and praying with them—was a moving experience for me. I often went to a room at the beginning of the week to find an empty bed and discover that the patient had died over the weekend. Being a chaplain taught me much about the fragile nature of life and about the longing in every person to experience release from pain and fear when death is imminent.

It has been said that most of us are not aware of good health while we have it. It is only when sickness sets in that we realize the wonder and beauty of health.

I know there have been times in my life when I have longed for a release from a wracking virus or a hacking cough. Being confined to bed not only hobbles my body, but wrecks me emotionally and mentally. I want to get well just so I can think clearly. I long for an uninterrupted sleep.

A flu bug can paralyze our powers of reason and set us on edge. When health returns—the easy breathing and the restful sleep—we feel so overcome with relief that our sighs are almost prayers.

Enjoying our good health involves far more, however, than just being healthy. Health is not simply the absence of sickness, but the presence of vibrancy, energy, life. Getting the most out of ourselves is every bit as much an indicator of good health as is the absence of measles or chicken pox. When we feel good about ourselves, when we awake refreshed in the morning, eager to face the challenges of a new day, that is health. When we enjoy what we do and look forward to tomorrow, we walk the road of wellness.

One evening several years ago, I received an unexpected phone call from a local substance abuse center. The director of that facility asked if I might visit a young man who was soon to be released. Evidently, as part of the therapy, the director and doctors there considered a final act of confession to be integral to the healing process. I set an appointment with the young man for the following morning but did not sleep well that night, fearful of what I might encounter in this new experience.

When I arrived at the center, an aide escorted me through a series of bolted doors to a private seating area at the rear. After a few minutes of waiting, a young man shuffled into the room and took a seat directly across from me. Doors were closed. And he began to speak.

Of course, I will not reveal what was said in the confession, but I was amazed at the amount of emotional and psychological baggage the young man had been carrying. He wept, he shouted, he padded around the room and beat his chest on several occasions. There were moments when, after uttering some deep, dark secret of the soul, he sighed so heavily I could feel the breath from his body. He talked nearly nonstop for over an hour, jumping from one detail to the next, his mannerisms and body language growing calmer with every passing minute, with each admission of guilt and shame and longing for love.

I felt as if I were watching a boxing match. Only in this case, a single man pummeled himself with blow after blow. When, at long last, he said his final word, I could see that a great calm had entered him and that he was on the road to recovery. It was as if years of torment and anguish had somehow been released from his body, all the pain and feelings of guilt somehow torn from his heart.

Watching that young man go through his ordeal, I realized he would never have achieved health without talking about his history and his problems. This confession may have been the first and only time in his life that he had talked about his anguish and guilt with another person. He was reaching for health by reaching out to someone else.

Take the time to practice a bit of healthy living by following this lead. When you are vexed by problems and concerns, find a friend who is a good listener. Lean upon someone else for support and understanding. Unresolved strains and worries have a way of showing up in our bodies sooner or later. Chronic headaches, backaches, sleeplessness, fatigue—all of these can be caused by carrying our worries like a badge of honor. A great many physical ailments vanish when we find peace of mind.

In the course of my life, I have been abundantly blessed with good health. I don't know why. I've never fallen from a tree and broken a bone; never spent a day in the hospital in my life; never been on any medication (other than for flu and colds) for an extended period of time. I've had few aches and pains.

When I think about why this is so given all the opportunities my life has presented for bodily harm, I have to think that either I've been incredibly lucky, or I enjoy a high tolerance for pain and possess a knack for avoiding trouble. Maybe it's a bit of both.

You and I not only desire good health, we want to enjoy it. But possessing a vibrancy for life is never easy. We have to work at it. And we have to think about it. That's why, every year when Easter rolls around, I take a lesson from Mr.

Barrington, a farmer-philosopher who taught me much about life and health and the joy of living.

Every year come Easter time, Mr. Barrington would drag himself and his wife out of the refreshing Florida sunshine and head north for another try at raising chickens. He had three huge chicken houses that spanned the distance between his house and back pasture, and each of these could hold something like a thousand pullets. Mr. Barrington always made a point of inviting me over a few weeks prior to Easter so I could see his newest shipment of chicks when they came in.

I was there one spring day when the delivery trucks came rumbling up the drive—massive wire-lined trailers loaded with peeping yellow chicks. One by one, the trucks backed against the chicken houses, opened their chutes and drained the chicks out of the truck beds like yellow cement pouring from a spout. The baby chicks huddled together in massive groups like amoebas, looking lost and bewildered inside their new spacious home. The sound of their peeping was so loud that all other noises, even voices, were quelled in their wake.

Mr. Barrington, his face tanned and healthy-looking from his days in the Florida sun, always stood at the door of each chicken house, gazing proudly at his newest batch of infants. Then, as soon as the trucks backed out of the drive, he would hand me a snow shovel and the two of us would enter the chicken houses to collect the chicks that didn't make it. The first time I helped with this task, I was amazed at the number of dead or dying chicks littering the floor. But Mr. Barrington always talked the same line as we went about the work.

"Folks are a lot like chickens," he'd say. "Only we don't know it. We get dumped into this world, and, at first, it's a mighty strange place. Most of us don't know what to make of it all. We're scared. So we huddle in groups, and form our own little societies and prejudices and opinions that make us feel quite good about ourselves, and quite uncertain of the other guy. But all the while, we're being fed and watered, going about our business. We're in our own little group, and we don't even know that the other groups exist. Or maybe we don't care. We're growing, and getting older and bigger, but we're not aware of these realities. We just peck away, strutting our new feathers and believing that we are the best of the brood, unaware that all of this, one day, is going to come to an end.

"Some get lost on the way into this world and bow out early. Maybe they are the luckiest ones. The rest of us keep pecking away. When there is not enough to go around, or when the house gets a bit crowded, or when our space is invaded, then we start pecking at each other. If we draw blood, we peck all the harder until the weakest among us are subdued and expire. We don't like those who are not like us or are not a part of our little groups. We feel like we've accomplished something grand and glorious for ourselves when we bring another down.

"Finally, when the time comes, we go out the same way we came in. But instead of going down the chute, we're going up the chute. But by the time we know it, it's too late to do anything about it, and we find that we haven't done a thing except eat and sleep and drink and peck and take up space."

Mr. Barrington would finish this diatribe with a flourish, a smile on his face—a farmer-philosopher. Then he'd turn to deliver the punch line. "Best to enjoy life while you've got it, son," he'd tell me. "As long as you've got your youth and your good health, make hay while the sun is shining. Don't just take up space. Make your life count for something, or for somebody else. Because someday the truck is coming for us both, and we're going up the chute."

I understood what he was saying. But I don't think I'd ever heard it quite that way before, although his analogy made perfect sense.

Mr. Barrington enjoyed his health, and he knew how to live well. He gave himself away. I saw this in the fashion he talked and ate and strutted and flexed. He was one glorious rooster.

Every year, on Easter Sunday, he would cart a box of healthy yellow chicks to the worship service and give them to the children. He'd hand them out like oranges or candy, and he'd say, always within earshot of the parents, "Happy Easter! Have a chick. Take it home and learn. And may God bless you with a long and healthy life."

14

Memories

And the tear that we shed, though in secret it rolls,
Shall long keep memory green in our souls.

—Thomas Moore

I don't usually talk to strangers, especially older women in nursing facilities, but this lady caught my eye. Or, I should say, she caught me! She reached right out and took me by the arm as I tried to exit the building.

"Come over here," she told me from her electric wheelchair. "I want to show you something." She led me down the hallway, steering with one hand and squeezing my forearm so tightly with the other that her grip felt like a vise. I guess she didn't want me to get away like all the others. I considered bolting, but relaxed when I realized she was smiling at me. Besides, I knew I would feel guilty withholding my arm from a woman old enough to be my grandmother—and then some.

I looked up and down the hallway. Not a nurse in sight. No one to come to my rescue. I had no choice but to proceed. Peeking at her name tag, I noted that her name was Dorothy; no last name. Evidently we were already on a first-name basis.

She led me into her room—a tidy cubicle littered with window plants, a pile of opened greeting cards and assorted letters, a dusty television in one corner. She sidled up to the bed and pointed to a nearby chair.

When she released her grip, I pulled away and sat down. The room had a stale odor, though tinged with the sterile aroma of freshly sprayed disinfectant. I leaned forward and put my elbows on my knees in anticipation of a quick exit.

Dorothy stared at me for a moment. "You're a good-looking young man," she said, a twinkle in her eye. She leaned closer to me.

So, this is what she has in mind? I thought. Nervously, I settled into the chair, tabloid headlines streaking across my brain: Young Man Has Secret Affair with Ninety-Five-Year-Old Sex Goddess; Local Grandma Lures Unsuspecting Stud into Sex Lair; "He Was My First!" Claims Sex-Starved Nonagenarian.

"How old are you?" Dorothy asked, pulling her wheelchair a bit closer.

"I'm . . . uh, well . . . errr," I stammered.

"You old enough to remember honeydippers?"

"Excuse me?"

"Honeydippers!"

What were they? I wondered. *A rock and roll group from the sixties? Some type of eating utensil?* I could only shrug in ignorance.

"Honeydippers," she continued, "were the fellows that came around every so often to clean the outhouse pit."

"Oh," I admitted. "No. That was a little before my time."

"Never mind," Dorothy said. There was an awkward silence as Dorothy continued to inspect me. "What's your name?"

I introduced myself. But my name seemed to confuse her all the more. Dorothy stared at me, searching my eyes for something, or someone. "Are you Manny's boy?" she asked eventually.

"No," I told her.

"Then you don't remember Manny?"

"Sorry, I don't."

"You're not old enough to remember Manny, are you?"

Suddenly a nurse flashed into the room, breaking up the awkward conversation. She placed a fresh set of towels on the end of the bed then came around behind Dorothy and gave me a wink. "I see Dorothy got ahold of you," she said.

I nodded, smiled, tried to act casual.

The nurse patted the old woman on the shoulder. "Don't let him get away, Dorothy," she said. "You finally got a man in your room."

Dorothy glanced back at the nurse. "He doesn't remember Manny."

The nurse waited, then came around to whisper in my ear. "Some days she's worse than others. Her son claims she doesn't remember him half the time, but she can remember fifty years ago like it was yesterday."

"Manny's my son," Dorothy said loudly.

"That's right," the nurse affirmed. "Manny's your son. You're having a good day."

As soon as the nurse left, Dorothy pointed to a small chest of drawers. "I want to show you my things," she said. "My things are down there."

Noticing that she wanted me to open the bottom drawer, I obeyed. I walked the couple of steps to the chest of drawers and tugged at the lowest set of handles. The scent of moth balls rose from the interior of the chest and drew my attention to a bulging packet of envelopes bound with a thick rubber band. I held up the mass of papers and asked, "Is this what you want?"

Dorothy pointed again to the chair. "Those are my things. Sit down so I can show them to you."

Realizing that I was in for a long siege, I handed the packet to Dorothy, sat down and braced myself for the worst. She removed the rubber band, pulled out a yellowed photo, and then began to reminisce in a style that, at first, made my skin crawl, but later became something of a delight. "This is me. My father owns the grist mill, and I help out every day after school. We have horses and a cow. Some chickens. My mother . . . this is her right here . . . bakes wonderful pies. Apple mostly. Some cherry. This Sunday we are going to visit my uncle on the farm. Of course, we will go to church first. That is one of Papa's rules. Always go to church on Sunday.

"This is a picture of my brother. He's a Presbyterian, and is going to come and take me home someday. Then we are going to dance. We always dance when we get together, and he is a great kidder.

"See, here is my horse. Her name is Ginger. She got loose last week, and Papa had to tie her up in the barn."

Dorothy continued to pull photos from the bundle, each time telling me the story of her life as if it were happening in the present moment. She was a little girl again, frolicking in the fields, riding her horse, helping her papa in the grist mill. There was nothing but happiness in her voice.

At last she pulled from the bundle a collection of poems she had written on the backs of envelopes and pieces of scrap paper. They were a kind of Dickinsonian collection, a secret volume of her life, full of the feelings and passions of a woman who had lived with energy and hopes. She did not read her poems, but handed them to me one by one, as if I were to interpret their meaning and find within the words the pieces of her life that she had left behind as a legacy to the world.

I did read. And I found Dorothy inside the words. She was still there, all of her, although the present had somehow lapsed into the past and the little girl had become the elderly woman. She seemed almost embarrassed when I commented favorably about her poems and handed them back.

Slowly, over the course of minutes, she stacked the individual photos and bits of paper, bound them with the rubber band, and placed them in her lap. When she looked up, she seemed startled to see me sitting in the chair across from her. She gazed at me hard. "Are you Manny?" she asked.

"No," I said. "I'm not Manny."

"Are you my son?"

I cleared the knot in my throat. What was I to say? "I would like to be your son," I told her.

Dorothy smiled and seemed satisfied by my answer. I leaned over and gave her a soft kiss on the cheek. She said nothing as I stepped away and exited the room.

Down the hallway, as I brushed past the nurses' station, the same nurse beckoned to me and offered an apology for

Dorothy. But none was needed. "I was afraid she was going to keep you for a while," she said. "When she gets someone in her room, she can go on for hours."

"No problem," I said. "She showed me some of her photos and poems. I think she thought I was her son."

The nurse didn't respond right away. She glanced back at Dorothy's room. "Around here we have a saying: Sometimes memories are the only things that keep people alive."

Yes, that nurse was correct: Memories can do that. They can be that, even for people who have no concept of today—maybe *especially* for them.

What would you and I do without our memories? Where would we go when we are lonely, when our love is running low, if not to the storehouse of the mind? Our memories define us. They tell us who we are, where we have come from. Memories attach themselves to the mind and hold us to the ones who love us. Through our memories we can always go back to that moment when life was simpler, when love was fresh and new. We can return to the grist mill, to the meadow, to the childhood days of old. And we can hearken back to the first love, the first kiss, that one moment in the sun.

Oh, we have these memories—or at least we have the longing for such things.

But memories don't need to be sentimental or childish to be powerful. Most of our memories are bolder, sharper. Memories are the mortar of life. They hold us together when times are tough, give us an anchor when we are uncertain of the future. Sometimes those memories help sustain us, or give us joy, or make us laugh.

In essence, our memories compose us; they make us who we are. They are the stories of our life.

When you and I recall events from childhood—a favorite moment, the face of a loved one—we do not just remember snippets of time. We remember people, happenings, movement. Our memories are verbs, not nouns. They are stories. Our memories compose the narratives that make up our lives.

It has been said that we are the only beings on earth who know that we have a past. We also know that we will die. In between is how we live.

Memories are, however, much different than nostalgia. Nostalgia has about it an otherworldly quality that says, "Life back then was better than today." Nostalgia denies that our childhoods, our adolescent years, our marriages and jobs and dreams were and are filled with difficulties and sometimes pain. Nostalgia has a somewhat unreal quality.

But life is never this neat, this carefree. As M. Scott Peck wrote at the beginning of his bestselling book, *The Road Less Traveled*: "Life is difficult." Those three words epitomize life as we know it.

Memories, however, never shy away from the pain and struggles of the past. Without our memories of such times, we would have no learning experiences upon which to draw. We would forever repeat the same mistakes over and over again. A good memory tells us: "Life is going to be better tomorrow because I know I have overcome the struggles of yesterday."

An old friend of mine (old in the sense of being *old*) named Bob is always quick to point out that if nostalgia were an accurate representation of life, we would have no reason to go on living.

"Folks who talk about the good old days don't remember too well," he always says. "I lived those days, and I can tell you there's no way anyone would want to go back to driving a horse and buggy on dirt roads or hauling in water from a well on a winter day. My wife could no more do without her microwave oven and telephone than she could her car or electric iron. I remember when we had none of these things, and I'm here to tell you—today is better than yesterday!"

I appreciate people like Bob, who remind me that I cannot live in the past—no matter how hard I try. The world just keeps on changing. I might as well change with it.

In fact, it's people from the generation born during or immediately following the Great Depression who have changed the most in American history! Think about it. Everything this generation of people has known in life has changed: transportation, communication, the conveniences of home. They have gone from horse and buggy to moon walks and space stations orbiting the earth. They have gone from telegraph to telephone. They've gone from cooking over open fires in the hearth to cooking in microwave ovens. When I consider all of these changes, the people of my grandparents' generation amaze me. I only hope that I can do so well adapting to the inevitable changes that will take place in my lifetime.

When I know people like Bob, who have their vast storehouse of memories intact and also drive a luxury automobile, I feel inspired to remember well, too. Memories that teach and heal and nourish are the finest memories of all.

Hearkening back to my own early years, I have many fantastic memories. Most of these have a surrealistic quality to them. For example, when I recall something of my child-hood, I do not recall the memory through the eyes and mind of the child I was *then*. I recall the memory through the eyes and mind of the adult I am *now*. I see myself as a boy stand-ing at home plate, awaiting the pitch, driving the ball into left field. I do not actually see the ball coming toward me, nor the ball springing off the end of the bat. As I have talked to people and listened to others talk about their pasts, I believe this reality is true for most. This is *how* we remember.

Memories relegate us to characters in a drama—our own drama, to be sure—but a drama nevertheless. Our memories are narratives, as if we were watching ourselves on a movie screen or reading about ourselves in a novel. Each moment that we recall has a face, a name, a movement, a sound. We hear what we *think* we heard *then*.

Of course, this is why memory is such a fragile and fleeting thing. Put two people on a courtroom witness stand and ask them what they saw two months ago when the accident occurred: the court is likely to hear differing versions of the same event. Why? Because there *were* two versions of the same event—two different sets of eyes, two different vantage points, two different minds working out the meaning of the event. This is why, if you've ever served on a jury, it is required that jurors be able to bring these pieces of the puzzle together to form a composite picture of an occurrence. All memories are interpretations.

Although our memories are selective and sketchy, how-ever, they do give us great comfort. I realize this fact every time I visit an individual or a family who has recently lost a loved one.

Grief usually extracts the best memories we hold inside. When people talk about the people they have loved and lost, they find celebration and happiness in the little things. They might remember a family vacation, a summer evening on the porch, a humorous anecdote. These memories are spiritual treasures, like the lingering presence of the one who has died.

Normally, before I conduct a funeral service, I like to sit down with the family in the home and ask about the one who has died. What kind of a person was she? What do you remember most about her?

Inevitably the family tells their stories. Sometimes scrapbooks are removed from cabinets, books are read, a host of memories come flooding back. Usually, even in the midst of the sadness of the moment, there is laughter, as family members recall happy times, joyous occasions, treasured moments. Sometimes folks make statements like, "I loved the way she laughed" or "She had the brightest smile of anyone in the family."

Grief often brings out the best memories. And these memories give us comfort.

In the past few years, I've also seen a renewed interest among families in displaying photos at a funeral service. These photo displays are an excellent way for people to deal with their loss and to remember the unique qualities of the individual. Many funeral homes now produce videotapes to serve this same purpose, to provide families an opportunity to view pictures, home movies and other images of their loved one.

Grief is a necessary component of healing when we lose someone we love. But sharing our memories is also a wonderful healing mechanism.

As with people, we often attach memories to things. In my attic I keep a box filled with the trappings of my childhood: a piece of basketball net our team won in a grade-school tournament; a baseball trophy I received when I was nine years old; glass marbles; a textbook; high school year books; a few letters. My wife also has a collection of her memories. So do most of the people I know.

I suppose all have a need, not only to remember where we have come from, but also to pass along a small piece of ourselves to our children and our grandchildren. We can find beauty and joy in these small things—maybe an old baseball glove or a china doll.

Most families enjoy passing along heirlooms from one generation to the next—perhaps a favorite chest of drawers or a book, or even jewelry. Sharing these heirlooms gives us a feeling of connection with our ancestors. In some small way, our loved ones live on through these memories—these hand-me-downs that are passed from one generation to the next. Such memories should be celebrated and enjoyed.

Memories themselves are such an important aspect of family life. The sheer fun and joy that can be found in the daily affairs of living are what children remember. Isn't it true that we remember best those things that we do with the most regularity? Don't we recall with more intensity those moments established early in life as important to the family and our well-being?

When families establish rituals, have fun together and enjoy all the little things together, there can be no doubt that some powerful memories will be established. Children and parents alike will remember many of the same times, places and moments of laughter.

In my family, I know my parents and brother remember many of the same great moments. We have memories of vacations together, can retell many of the same hilarious stories, and relish equally those funny moments when something went awry—like the time the pet goat got loose and we searched the town for hours, only to find him sitting on the neighbor's porch across the street.

I hope my children will have many fond memories of their early years. I want them to recall the love and strength we shared as a family and the hurdles they were able to overcome in school, in friendships and in meeting new people. It has been said if we want our children to be strong adults, we must allow them to experience and overcome hardship as children (with active parental love and support, of course). A soft childhood produces a soft adult.

Pleasant memories provide children, as they grow older, a history of strength. They will understand that they are loved; they will know that they have the gifts and emotional resources to be whatever they want to be. Strong memories will make *them* strong.

This emotional history is one of the reasons that memories serve us well as we grow older. It is also the reason, I suppose, that many people in the twilight of life find more happiness by living in the past than in the present moment. They were strong and vibrant back then (in the old days). All the people they knew and loved best were gathered around. It is no wonder that many people hang on to their memories with such ferocity as they grow older.

The clincher in this memory game, I suppose, is keeping our memories alive without losing our identities and our zest for life. We have a past, but we know we can't live there. We have to live in the present moment. And tomorrow may never come. Memories may refresh and teach, but we must master them if we are to create a future.

This becomes difficult for us at the point where our unpleasant memories keep us from embracing each new day with expectation and joy. We all have these memories: recollections of dear friends and family members who have died; moments when someone hurt us or betrayed our trust; times when we felt unloved and abandoned. If we allow these unpleasant memories to consume our minds and hearts, the refreshing memories have no room to help us grow.

That is why many people learn to use their past sorrows and pains as a creative outlet. Many paintings, poems, novels and songs have a sad quality to them—but they can also refresh and inspire. Blues music and much of country music are creative outlets for the sadness we often associate with the past. But we find that, when we paint, or sing or write about our blues, these sorrows no longer have control of us; they cease to have the power to consume us.

In 1896, a British poet named Alfred Edward Housman published a slim volume of poetry entitled *A Shropshire Lad*. This collection of verse contained a few dozen melancholy poems that addressed the brevity of life and the frailty of human love. The book was an immediate success and is still in print today.

One of A. E. Housman's poems, "With Rue My Heart Is Laden," contains the kind of melodrama we often associate with remembering childhood friends:

With rue my heart is laden
For golden friends I had,
For many a rose-lipped maiden
And many a lightfoot lad.

By brooks too broad for leaping
The lightfoot boys are laid;
The rose-lipped girls are sleeping
In fields where roses fade.

When we have the blues, finding a creative outlet for our painful memories may be just the thing we need. Some folks find comfort in keeping a journal or diary of such feelings and memories. Others like to sing about them. Some like to surround themselves with artifacts that remind them of these memories—antiques and keepsakes that are a source of comfort and serve as reminders of the past.

Even our painful memories are a blessing to us. They are as much a part of life as the pleasant remembrances.

Charles Dickens understood this very well. Critics of his writing have long understood that many of Dickens's novels are semiautobiographical in nature. Through such novels as *David Copperfield* and *Nicholas Nickleby*, Dickens dealt with the pain and sorrow of his own unhappy childhood. Writing these novels freed him from the demons of his own past.

Although best known for his novels, Dickens did write a number of short stories as well. One such story, "Tale of a Chemist," is particularly noteworthy.

In this futuristic tale, a famous chemist is tortured by the painful memories of his past. He tries desperately to shake these memories from his mind, recollections that haunt him, plague his days and torment his nights. But his efforts are to no avail.

Eventually he decides that he will undergo a series of experimental shock treatments, which will obliterate his memory and give him a new lease on life. This he does, and the shock treatments are a complete success.

However, the chemist soon discovers that the obliteration of his memory has had some dire consequences. Because his entire memory has been erased, he has no past. He cannot remember where he was born, who his parents were, who his friends are or where he has come from. He is lost without the simple recollections of familiar faces and names. Not only the painful memories are gone, but also the memories that compose his identity as a human being.

At the end of the story, the chemist cries out for his past—painful memories and all. He wants what he has lost, for without his memories he is nothing. Wilting inside, he cries out again and again, "Keep my memory green. Keep my memory green."

Dickens understood that one of life's greatest blessings is the power of memory. Without a history, we are lost. Without the ability to recall where we have come from and what we have experienced in life's depths and peaks, we are little more than shadows.

Keeping our memory green is not always easy. But remembering well is one of the keys to living well. Our memories are truly blessings. And better yet, no one can take them from us. Memories are one of the few things we truly own.

Cherishing memories—moments of laughter and joy and hope, moments of family and friendship—these can last us a lifetime. Memories are some of the best and brightest gifts.

Perhaps this is what the apostle Paul had in mind when he wrote these beautiful words from a prison cell nearly two thousand years ago:

> *Finally . . . whatever is true, whatever is honorable, whatever is just, whatever is pure, whatever is pleasing, whatever is commendable, if there is any excellence and if there is anything worthy of praise, think about these things. Keep on doing the things that you have learned and received and heard. . . . and the God of peace will be with you.*

> —Phil. 4:8–9 NRSV

15

Rest

Time is infinite movement without rest.

—Leo Tolstoy, *War and Peace*

Among the many Christian traditions and stories worth retelling are those attributed to the Desert Fathers. And among these, one tale goes like this: Once some pilgrims came to see Father Poemen. They asked him, "If a brother goes to sleep during the sacred readings and prayers, what should we do? Pinch him, so he will stay awake?" Father Poemen answered, "On the contrary. If I saw a brother sleeping, I would place his head upon my knees and let him rest."

I like this story because it reminds me that rest is an essential element of life. When we are weary and worn, it is among the sweetest of life's pleasures. While it may be said we were born to work and sweat and strive against great odds, it is equally true that rest is the joy we anticipate when all of our

striving is accomplished and the long shadows of day have
stretched into twilight. Rest is the gift of a free day, a long
afternoon, a moment in the sun. We long to put our feet up,
dangle in the hammock, sit in the shade of the old oak on a
Sunday afternoon in the wake of a ferocious picnic lunch.

We find these restful moments difficult to enjoy, I suppose,
because we are so driven, so geared for activity rather than
relaxation. So many of us find it difficult to slow down, to
take things easy. We imagine that every day was created for
some personal achievement.

Rest may not be what we want. But rest is what we need.

Years ago, when I was studying for the ministry, I worked
alongside an older pastor for several weeks to watch and learn
from him. Every day this pastor rose early, read the morning
newspaper over several cups of steaming black coffee, and
then went about his business—visiting the sick and lonely,
making hospital calls, preparing sermon notes. Every day was
filled with unique challenges and difficulties—with one
exception.

Every afternoon, following a light lunch, this older pastor
retired to his living room couch, slipped off his shoes, and
reveled in a thirty-minute nap. Naturally, being younger and
more energetic, I was climbing the walls during this rest ses-
sion. I wanted to get out and get going again. I scarcely had
time for this relaxed atmosphere. Eventually I found the confidence to ask the pastor about his little habit.

"Oh, I've been taking an afternoon nap since I was a boy,"
he told me. "My mother taught me that rest is an important
ingredient of the day, and I've heeded her advice ever since.
I think you'd do well to get into the habit also. I find that a

little nap in the afternoon refreshes me, keeps my mind focused on the important things and keeps me from burning out. After all, I took up this pastor's gig for the long haul. And I've found that few things in life are truly emergencies, even when people think you ought to do something *now*. Oh, you'll live a lot longer and with less worry if you take a daily nap."

Perhaps this is the tradition and reasoning behind the afternoon siesta and the easygoing philosophy one typically finds in other cultures, particularly in Latin countries. While we in America find it difficult to rest, the afternoon respite is a moment to be honored in other cultures. We still have much to learn from those who have found time to rest in the midst of life's busyness.

A friend of mine recently returned from a work project in Jamaica and noted this same phenomenon there. Working side by side with the Jamaican people, my friend discovered that, as an American, he was most concerned with doing: completing the job, forging ahead, trying to make good time on the project before the sun went down. But to the Jamaican people, these concerns were secondary. They were more concerned with being: enjoying the moment, talking with friends, laughing. My friend noted that the Jamaican people seemed to live with a greater degree of satisfaction and light-hearted tranquillity than most Americans.

One of the favorite expressions of the Jamaican men is "Take it easy, mon!" Every time my friend fell into a tizzy from wondering when the lumber shipment was coming in or grew weary from worrying about the next day's project, he was greeted with smiles.

"Relax! Take it easy, mon!"

The message was clear: Don't get upset. Enjoy the moment. The sun will rise tomorrow. Just be content to *be*!

These differences are worth noting. We typically gauge our self-worth and our value by what we accomplish. But others find their value in being and belonging.

Some years ago, Paul Tillich, a noted Christian theologian, wrote a slim volume of sermons entitled *The Courage to Be*. In his book, he addresses this human struggle to find meaning in recreation and rest, this yearning to be at peace with ourselves. Funny how we search for meaning through so many different venues and yet consistently discover that we are restless to the bone. We can't wait for tomorrow and, consequently, we miss the wondrous experiences of today. I see this restlessness in myself, and I wonder where it comes from.

Yes, I need rest. So do you. But where do we go when we need it?

Perhaps Silvia Lyons has an answer. She oversees a home for teenage girls in northern Indiana and also manages a private retreat center. From her vantage point, she sees many people who are broken and distraught. She helps those who need to find their lives again. But more than that, she has found that her retreat center is increasingly used by business professionals and average men and women who are in desperate need of rest and renewal. Some just need a place where they can get away from the demands that have been placed upon their lives. Others yearn for peace of mind.

I heard Sylvia speak one day to a group concerning our human confusion and our preoccupation with possessions. She talked about the need to surround ourselves with simplicity and silence instead of clutter and noise. Sometimes we find our rest only when we withdraw from the familiar, from the accumulation of things that we equate with "the good life."

Indeed, rest may be found as easily in a life of simplicity and frugality as in a retreat center. We don't have to back-pack into the wilderness to find quiet. We can find it within. Or, to put it another way, rest is what we find when we are able to free our hearts and minds from life's complexities and demands. Relaxation and peace come when we are un-encumbered by worries, cares and anxieties. We experience rest when we are at peace with ourselves.

Among the many religious traditions of the world, Zen Buddhism, perhaps, speaks most clearly of this need to find inner tranquillity, this rest that comes when we are at peace with ourselves and at one with the world. A Zen parable worth retelling at this juncture begins in this manner:

> Once there was a man who was earnestly seeking enlighten-ment. He was known far and wide for his devotion and his striv-ing. In order to hasten his attainment of enlightenment, he fasted and prayed, meditated day and night. Likewise he grew thinner and weaker, even to the point where others began to comment on his noticeable progress.
>
> Eventually the master of the temple approached the fellow and asked, "Why are you in such a hurry? What is your rush?"
>
> The fellow said, "I seek enlightenment and time is wasting."
>
> But the master responded, "And how do you know that you will find enlightenment by rushing ahead, as if it were before you? Perhaps enlightenment is behind you, and you will find it by standing still."

In our modern haste to make every moment count, I won-der whether we have not overlooked the simple peace that comes from taking a moment for ourselves, from standing still and seeking a moment of inner rest. The Jewish prophets spoke of humble living and simple devotion to God. Buddhist sages admonished their adherents to forget the self. Jesus taught his disciples not to worry about the future, nor to grow anxious concerning daily necessities such as clothing, food and drink. All of these lead to rest for the weary spirit and give us peace.

Sometimes we find rest when we are looking for it. Other times rest comes to us through the unexpected moments of life.

Such is the case when there's a baby in the house. Not mine, necessarily, but anyone's.

Have you ever noticed how tranquil adults become when they hold a newborn? A big macho guy sits down on the couch, a baby is placed into his arms, and the next thing you know, he's snoring away. The man, not the baby. I think there must be something to all this touchy-feely stuff, something to the notion that warmth and relationship are necessary ingredients in life. We have a need to be needed.

The same phenomenon can take place after an arduous hike up a mountain, or a strenuous bike ride through the countryside. We get to the top or to the end, and we pause. And in the pausing we suddenly realize that we are surrounded by an indescribable beauty and peace. We sigh. We are surprised by an unexpected gift of rest.

Or have you ever worked so hard at a project that, at the end of it all, you were so pleased with yourself that you felt this sudden peace flooding in? Or have you ever awakened early in the morning, your heart racing with the anticipation of going to work, only to discover that it is Saturday and you get to sleep in? Have you ever been reading the newspaper obituaries when suddenly you were aware of all that is good and meaningful in your life? These, too, are moments of unexpected rest.

Over the course of my life, it is amazing how many people I've known who have retired for one reason or another—some because they felt they had obtained financial security, others because they were ready for a lifetime of golf—only to discover that retirement was not the type of rest they were looking for. Some found that they had to stay active to stay alive. Others found that rest is not the same thing as retirement.

One fellow I know became so confused by his early retirement that he couldn't decide where he wanted to live. A part of him longed for the sunshine and wide-open spaces of southern Texas, a small ranch where he could sit around and count flies until the sun went down behind the cacti. But another part of him longed to take a part-time job working with children in his hometown. This was his immediate struggle. But the biggest part of himself wanted to find a different kind of rest than he had originally anticipated.

In the end his heart won out over his ranch, and he found that he could sleep better at night knowing that he had made a difference to a child.

There's that kind of rest—rest as internal satisfaction. That is the rest that comes to us when we know we are living well and all of our energies are focused on making the most of the day. Everyone needs to experience this rest now and again. It keeps us going strong. It makes us happy.

And then there is the rest for the weary.

When I was in seminary, I recall going to a soup kitchen one afternoon to help with the meal preparation. There was one fellow there, one of the helpers, who seemed to have rolled out of the wrong side of the bed that morning. He kept going on and on about how lazy some people were. "Look at those people out there," he'd say, "lining up for a free meal. Always wanting a handout. You don't think they're lazy?"

Finally another helper spoke up. "I don't see any lazy people out there," he said. "All I see are people who are weary to the bone, tired from all the burdens they've been carrying, and they've stopped by this place to rest."

I had a similar observation about life when I was a teenager.

Each year as Christmas approached, groups from our church went from house to house singing carols. We'd make a list of all the people in our community who had experienced some loss in their lives or were carrying heavy burdens, and we'd go and sing to them.

One particular Christmas that stands out in my mind was the year my group visited three homes, all of which had been touched by some recent tragedy. We caroled to a woman, recently widowed, who stood at the frosted window in her nightgown and wept as we sang about the peace of Bethlehem and the love that came down at Christmas. Afterward she gave us cookies and hot chocolate, but her face was creased with lines of worry and dread.

We caroled to an older couple about peace on earth and good news for the world. He was dying of cancer. She was wasting away in fear. And each of them longed for some unfathomable rest.

We also caroled at a home where the specter of death had visited, to a mother who had lost her teenage son to a drug overdose just weeks before. We sang "God Rest Ye Merry,

Gentleman," and there was something in the words that were of comfort to all who sang and to the mother who listened. Everyone, I believe, found rest that evening.

In the biblical story of creation, it is worth noting that rest comes at the end of all things. First comes the stuff of stars and galaxies and planets, followed by the parting of water and land. Next the vegetation. Then the creeping things, the fish and birds, the animals. At last human beings.

And then the creator rests.

According to the story, this rest is inherent in the ordering of creation itself: All things need to pause for station identification, for renewal, for life. Without the rest, there can be no celebration, no joy.

Rest, then, is the glue that holds all things together. Rest is the last thing, or the first thing, depending upon how you want to look at it. Rest is built into the fabric of our beings, and we have to have it if we wish to know whence we have come and to where we are returning.

Life suffers when we don't give rest its due. We suffer when we fail to pause for what is natural and needed. This is the rest promised to us from the beginning of time. It is the ultimate rest.

Years back, I recall having an exceptionally difficult funeral service to conduct. The woman who had died was a pillar of the community, a well-known and much-loved contributor in the church and schools. I had no difficulty finding the words, but something seemed lacking.

This woman had been a "doer" all of her life. She was involved in many activities, and seemed to have an unfailing spirit and energy that drove her day and night. Everyone understood that she worked hard and, because of her activity in so many functions, was going to be terribly missed. Some wondered how their respective organizations would fare without her help and talent.

It wasn't until we gathered around the casket at the cemetery that I discovered the appropriate ending to the funeral service. There, among the dying trees of autumn, the bold colors of sky and cloud, I spoke of this woman's passing and the belief that her work on earth was accomplished. She had done all that she could with her life. She had entered into a well-deserved rest.

Indeed, that is the promise. We shall rest from our labors, the Scriptures say. We shall find rest for our souls.

When all was completed and the last of the family was heading back to their cars, a young man approached to shake my hand. He seemed tranquil. There was a calmness in his demeanor.

"Hi. I'm the grandson," he told me. "Just flew in from Seattle this morning for the funeral. I wondered how I was going to make sense of my grandmother's death. She was the glue that held our family together. We knew we could always count on her. She was such a worker, always doing things for someone else; always active. And now she's gone.

"But I just wanted you to know, what you said back there about an eternal rest—I liked that. I liked that a lot. It sounds wonderful. And I want you to know . . . I could sure use some of that!"

Yes, I thought, *couldn't we all?*

ABOUT THE AUTHOR

Todd Outcalt has spent most of his life in his native Hoosier state of Indiana. He and his wife, Becky, have two children and make their home in Indianapolis. As a United Methodist pastor, Todd has served churches in Indiana and in North Carolina, and has worked closely with children and teenagers on numerous mission projects throughout the United States. He has also participated in archaeological work in Israel.

An author of several books and upcoming titles, Todd has also written for many national publications and is a contributing editor to *For the Bride* magazine, where his column, "Malebag," appears frequently. His books include *Before You Say "I Do," Meeting-Space Ideas for Youth Ministry* and *Seeing Is Believing.*

Todd continues to lead parenting, ministry and marriage workshops, and speaks to many groups each year.

For further information about seminars or to schedule

Todd for a speaking engagement, please contact him at:

8339 S. East Street
Indianapolis, IN 46227
phone: 317-859-6782
email: *teoutcalt@aol.com*